PRISONS IN ISRAEL

PRISONS IN ISRAEL

A Study of Policy Innovation

by

JOSEPH W. EATON

With a Preface by the Honorable Justice Haim H. Cohn
of the Supreme Court of Israel

UNIVERSITY OF PITTSBURGH PRESS

Copyright 1964 by University of Pittsburgh Press

Library of Congress Catalog Card Number 64-15288

To Helen

Who cheerfully endures a matrimonial life sentence at hard labor

Foreword

How might an ideal prison system be set up? This is the fundamental question of the prison reform movement. Among the unresolved issues is the place of prisons in the effort to control social deviants. Who should be incarcerated and for how long? What kind of offenses can be contained by alternates to imprisonment, fines or suspended sentences? What, in general, should be the program of treatment for different categories of law violators? Prisons are expensive to maintain. They keep dangerous persons out of circulation. They punish law violators. But many violators are discharged more antisocial than when they entered.

Criminologists concerned with these questions must use what scientific knowledge there is and apply their intuition when knowledge is insufficient for policy-making. No state can survive without enforcing its laws. But there is much uncertainty about how enforcement can best be accomplished. Should punishment fit the crime or the criminal? Reformers often must compromise their principles to meet compelling expediencies. Penal innovations may have to begin in old buildings, or they may be circumscribed by existing laws and police practices. The present is a function of the past and of hopes for the future. Reformers cannot begin from the beginning. All social institutions, including prisons, must be analyzed within such a social-historical framework.

But what happens when a prison system is started without compelling organizational antecedents? This occurred in Israel after independence was achieved. The country was free to discard the traditions, popular wisdom, and legal requirements of its former rulers. The new government included men well versed in the history of penology. They were knowledgeable about the pitfalls existing in penal systems. They comprehended that prisons are a palliative, not a cure for the control of criminals.

What kind of a prison system emerged when the task of planning was turned over to such men, steeped in the social sciences and in a humanitarian philosophy? Would prisons be dealt with in the same innovative spirit that characterizes so many of Israel's public affairs? With the purpose of answering these questions, the writer made a brief survey in 1962 of the development of penal policy in Israel. During two months, he visited every one of the country's six prisons, interviewed law-enforcement officials, judges, welfare workers, university professors and others. His observations were analyzed against the background of information recently derived from a study of penal reform in California.[1]

What are offered here are impressions. They are a basis for suggest-

1. Joseph W. Eaton, *Stone Walls Not a Prison Make: The Anatomy of Planned Administrative Change,* Springfield, Illinois: C. C. Thomas, Publisher, 1962.

ing organizational hypotheses. Their proof will have to await the collection of more conclusive evidence. The time available for field work was insufficient to pursue many interesting leads. Even in a country only slightly larger than the state of New Jersey, and much less populous, the penal system is a complex network of laws, people and administrative practices.

This study was financed by a faculty research grant from the Social Science Research Council. Help in the typing of field notes and in the preparation of the manuscript for publication was provided by Miss Barbara Caputo, Mr. Frederick A. Hetzel, Mrs. Dorothy S. Lederman and Dr. Helen Jean Moore.

The writer is indebted for much of what he learned to the candor, courtesy and critical capacities of his many informants. Officials of the prison system, especially Commissioner Aryeh Nir, Scientific Director Dr. Zvi Hermon, Warden A. Turgeman and Chief Social Worker Mrs. Victoria Nissim provided free access to, and much information about, the prison system. Dr. Menachem Amir and Lord Edwin Samuel critically reviewed the manuscript. All of them and many others contributed much from their intimate acquaintance with penology and Israel. But the conclusions offered here and the interpretations and the errors of this monograph are the writer's exclusive responsibility.

Preface

Any inquiry into the working and policy of a prison administration is of necessity closely bound up with an inquiry into administrative policies and orientations and the general makeup of the country concerned. Where the inquiry relates to a country governed by the rule of law and by democratic processes, there are, of course, some common denominators which may *a priori* be taken for granted: prisons will not, in such countries, be an end in themselves, but will be employed, in the ways and to the extent authorized by law, to attain some or all of the purposes of punishment. Still, the laws can never provide much more than the framework within which a large amount of discretion must be left to the policy-makers — first the judges and later the prison administrators; and it is not only the degree to which some purpose of punishment is eventually accomplished in respect of this or the other lawbreaker, but, more importantly, the ways and means employed to that end, and the spirit behind them, which mark the success or the failure of a prison administration.

To start an inquiry into the Israel prison system with the question, how might "an ideal prison system" be set up, as does the author of the present study, is — I am afraid — to raise expectations which neither the realities of the situation nor the conclusions at which the author himself arrives, can possibly justify. It is true that at the time of the establishment of the state and for some years thereafter, there were quite a number of ambitious idealists among us who would be content with nothing less than the "ideal" prison system; but, I am sorry to say, both their ambitions and their idealism in this respect suffered heavy and continuous blows from budgetary restrictions, on the one hand, and the pressure of alarmed, nay, often panicky public opinion, on the other hand. The result is a prison administration which has not, in fifteen years of statehood, attained any of the idealists' objectives; but it is no small consolation to have the exequatur of so outstanding an expert as the author of the present study, to the effect that we have fared no worse than many an older and a richer state.

The particular difficulties with which Israel has to cope, especially in regard to her heterogeneous prison population and her unique security problems, are instructively described in this book. As a matter of fact, they present a challenge worthy of thoughtful penologists all over the free world. We have been most fortunate, indeed, in attracting the interest of many renowned criminologists to whose advice and guidance we are deeply indebted. The author mentions the late Mr. Edmond Fitzgerald chief probation officer of Brooklyn, New York, and later a member of the state parole board. I should like, on my part, to take this opportunity to pay tribute to the memory of this most humane and scholarly of men, whose vision and confidence proved the most encouraging stimulus for us when we started to lay the first foundations for a penal system of our own, and whose untimely death deprived criminology of one of its best and most progressive practitioners.

As for us Israelis, the author very flatteringly divides us into two main categories: the military pioneers and the human relations specialists. May I express my apprehension that he is rather oversimplifying? As in most other countries, so in Israel a considerable portion of administrative policymaking is entrusted to officials who have no special qualifications for their jobs; in the course of their years of office they acquire such know-how and experience as they have. If this state of affairs is regrettable in all departments, it is doubly so in prison administration—and maybe even more so in regard to prison directors and wardens who have to carry the policy into effect, than in regard to the higher echelons of policymakers. There is, however, no solution to this problem: the civil service jobs are not attractive in terms of remuneration, prospects of a career are remote and slow, and the working conditions — especially in prisons and with prisoners — provide only an additional deterrent. The shortage of manpower, acute as it is in almost all departments, makes itself doubly felt in the prison service; and the few "military pioneers" and "human relations specialists" who hold out bravely can not make up for a well-trained and sufficiently qualified corps of prison staff. The best policies you may devise will be set at nought if the people who are available to carry them out are unwilling or unable to appreciate their purpose and act in their spirit. What is needed is not so much a mechanical obedience to the letter as rather a conscious desire to cooperate in the attainment of a common purpose. Personally, I am inclined to believe that in order to be successful you have to enlist even the help and cooperation of the prisoners themselves, or at least of a good majority of them; and, needless to say, without a prison staff that is in daily contact with them, you can never hope to achieve anything like such cooperation.

The "military pioneers" are, as their name implies, in the eyes of the author, apt to overemphasize the security aspect of prison administration; and inasmuch as they are at present "in power" in the prison administration, security aspects are overemphasized. Again, I venture to think this is oversimplifying matters. A prison is a place in which the law-abiding citizen expects his government to detain the lawbreakers in such a manner that they cannot possibly escape. It does not matter to the man in the street whether a criminal has been sent to prison for three months or ten years: so long as he is in prison by order of the court, he must emphatically be kept there and prevented from running away. It is true that prison escapes occur everywhere, even from highest security prisons; but I daresay that while the people of the United States, by and large, took the San Quentin and Alcatraz breaks with much equanimity, the Shatta prison break in Israel, nay, every individual prisoner's escape, caused a major uproar in Israeli public opinion. Some of the underlying reasons, mainly in the politico-strategical sphere, are well described in the present study; what I desire to stress here is that the emphasis on security on the part of the prison administration constitutes but a natural reflex to the popular sentiment and the official grant of a popular demand. I do not know that matters would be different if, instead of the "military pioneers," the "human relations specialists" were in power: the difference, if any, would be that the latter would have their *reservatio mentalis* that the policy they were pursuing was forced upon them by circumstances over which they have no control and by considerations not of their own making. Do I side with the "military pioneers" when I think that it is better to pursue a necessary policy wholeheartedly rather than with mental reservations?

This brings me to the question of prison policies in general. I should like to warn my readers at the outset that I am speaking as a judge and a lawyer, not as a prison administrator; and I may not be voicing the opinion of prison administrators when I say that prisons, as an institution for the enforcement of law, are an evil, the only justification for retaining them in our systems of law enforcement being the fact that so far no better substitute is available. But I firmly believe that in a humane and progressive community the use to be made of this necessary evil must be restricted to an absolute minimum: it should be used only as a last resort, when no other sanction is in any way likely to be instrumental in attaining one of the legitimate purposes of punishment. Needless to say, for such alternative sanction I rule out those punishments which to my mind are even more evil than imprisonment, such as capital or corporal punishments. Imprisonment has this in common with capital and corporal punishments, that *prima facie* it, too, is an encroachment on the dignity of man and on the inviolability of his person, and as such borders on the cruel and inhuman as outlawed in the Universal Declaration of Human Rights. The deprivation of a man's liberty necessarily implies the deprivation of his usual work, his family life, and all sorts of normal and legitimate amenities, of which to deprive a man is quite inconsistent with any notion of his dignity as a human being; and, what is worse, it inflicts great hardship and suffering on his spouse and children and parents, who must of course be presumed to be quite innocent of his misdeeds. I submit that the only crime situation in which no alternative sanction is available or effective, and imprisonment therefore legitimate, is where the public must by all means be protected from probably recurring acts of violence. Where the convicted prisoner is potentially dangerous, it does not matter whether he is in need of treatment (say for pathological impulses) or what his motives were: the society's right to be protected from him has priority over any of his "human" rights. It follows that the main purpose, and to my mind the only justification, of imprisonment is the protection of the public; hence it cannot be legitimate or justifiable where the public does not, from an objective point of view, require protection from a particular criminal, however much he deserves to be severely punished. That does not mean that it is not the duty of government to provide the maximum possible facilities in prisons for rehabilitation and treatment: if you can combine the necessary and the useful and put the period of imprisonment to good use for educational and reformatory purposes, so much the better. But it would mean indulging in a rather dangerous illusion, were we to pride ourselves that our prisons are, or are meant to be, model institutions of reform and rehabilitation, as if we were conferring on the prisoners the much-coveted pleasure or privilege of completing their civic education.

However all this may be, in actual practice (both of legislatures and of courts) imprisonment is virtually the standard punishment for crime in general. Fines are the exception, not the rule; and the cancellation of trading, driving, and similar licenses are incidental rather than primary sanctions. The author's statistical data on sentencing policy in Israel, which show a remarkable preference for suspended prison sentences and fines as distinguished from actual imprisonment, do not necessarily reflect, as the learned author opines, the traditional leniency of Jewish judges; however paradoxical it may sound, they reflect rather the state of the Israeli prisons. It is a fact that until a new women's prison was built a few years ago, there were practically no prison sentences at all handed down against female criminals: the judges knew very well the state of available accommodation for female prisoners, and unless they were compelled to do so by law (as in the case of murder, where life imprisonment is the obligatory sentence), they would not, in the exercise of their discretion, compel any woman to undergo this sort of imprisonment. The better the prisons are, the fewer the judges' inhibitions about imposing imprisonment; the worse the prisons are, the less likely is a conscientious judge to send a man to prison if he can possibly deal with him otherwise. For people like me who would like to have sentences of imprisonment reduced to an absolute minimum — would it not be better to keep our hands off any prison reform and let the prisons by their very inadequacy disprove and discredit themselves?

The answer is, of course, that society owes a duty even to those

xii

whom it must imprison for its protection. The duty is to reduce the evil of imprisonment to a minimum. It is true that the more successful you are in this respect, the easier will judges impose sentences of imprisonment. In Sweden, for instance, where prison reforms have attained unparalleled records, I found the prisons populated with traffic offenders, and most of them were rather cheerful about it. My own view is that traffic offenders, and particularly the recidivists and more dangerous among them, should have their driving licenses cancelled and be removed from the highways : prisons are no place for them. The same applies to all sorts of white-collar crime : depriving the criminal of the means to commit the offence again and of the fruits of his crime is a much better and fairer sanction, and a much more effective deterrent, than a period of imprisonment. But as there will always be men of violence from whom the society must be effectively protected, there is no choice but to maintain our prisons; and if we have to maintain them, let us try to find the synthesis between efficient security apparatuses and such places of human habitation as reflect the best of modern civilization.

On this, as on any problem arising in a free democracy, opinions in Israel as anywhere else may be divided; but, speaking for myself, I would wholeheartedly endorse for Israel what Winston Churchill once said as Home Secretary for Great Britain : "The mood and temper of the public in regard to the treatment of crime and criminals is one of the most unfailing tests of any country. A calm, dispassionate recognition of the rights of the accused and even of the convicted criminal, against the State, a constant heartsearching by all charged with the duty of punishment, a desire and eagerness to rehabilitate in the world of industry those who have paid their due in the hard coinage of punishment; tireless efforts towards the discovery of curative and regenerative processes; unfailing faith that there is a treasure, if you can only find it, in the heart of every man; these are the symbols which, in the treatment of crime and criminal, mark and measure the stored-up strength of a nation, and are sign and proof of the living virtue within it."

Israel stands just at the threshold of the storerooms she builds for her strength and virtues, in coming generations to unfold themselves. It is because of the indomitable will of a long-persecuted people to be free masters of their own destiny, and to take at long last their legitimate place among the free nations of the earth, that Israel is determined to make a success of independence and sovereignty; and her government and people are ambitious and idealistic enough not to fail the tests of civilization, and not to tire in their efforts to make life better and happier.

HAIM H. COHN
Supreme Court of Israel

Table of Contents

The Development of Penal Policy

Long-range planning, innovation and experimentation are deeply rooted in the renaissance of Israel. The foundations of a scientific land-reclamation program were laid in 1901 when the Jewish National Fund was established. Many of the country's early immigrants were trained in advance of their arrival for the new life that awaited them. A network of health and welfare agencies provided rehabilitative services that employed many of the world's most up-to-date practices. When the British high commissioner left Haifa on May 14, 1948, a Hebrew shadow government of specialists was ready. Its key personnel had worked together for decades. Imaginative men were ready to take over most of the technical functions of government. But there was no plan for a new prison system.

Prisons had played an insignificant role in the Jewish community before independence. The population had come to Israel on the basis of a highly selective immigration policy, and it was strongly identified with socialist and nationalist ideals. Jewish criminals were rare enough to be the objects of humor rather than of great concern.

Improvisation within a Planned Social System

Shortly after Israel declared its independence, a new prison was planned in a farming area near Tel Mond. Its capacity of 120 was hoped to be sufficient to meet the country's need. When this facility was opened on January 12, 1949, not quite seven months after the establishment of the state, there were only eighty-seven prisoners. A few weeks later, a general amnesty reduced that number to twenty-nine. "But before the rooms earmarked for workshops could be made use of as originally planned, there was a steep rise in the number of prisoners, and within a few months, it had passed the capacity mark. To meet the emergency, the workshops and dining room facilities which were to serve rehabilitative and cultural work had to be turned into cells, and the plan to build prison industries and to do cultural work had, for the time being, to be abandoned." [1]

1. Zvi Hermon, "The Israel Prison Service," *Treatment of Offenders in the State of Israel,* Tel Aviv: Government Printing Press, July, 1955, 57.
There are some quaint parallels in this account of Israel's first experience with prison reform and that of Walnut Street Prison in Philadelphia, America's first reform prison. It was opened shortly after the success of the American Revolution. Prison commitments dropped from 131 in 1789 to 45 in 1793. But initial enthusiasm shortly gave way to disillusionment. The prison became overcrowded by the turn of the century. It became harder to maintain good sanitary conditions. The industrial work program for inmates had to be discontinued. (Orlando F. Lewis, *The Development of American Prisons and Prison Customs 1776 to 1845. With Special Reference to Early Institutions in the State of New York,* New York: The American Prison Association, 1922, 38-42.

1

Worse was still to come. Infractions of the law increased steadily. In 1958, the most recent year for which full official statistics have been published, the services of 8,500 persons and the expenditure of large sums of money were required to deal with criminal matters. The police had 7,431 employees, including 487 in the prison service.[2] There were 122 judges and magistrates, although this figure includes those serving civil as well as criminal cases.

There had been no long-range planning for dealing with the emergence of criminal deviancy. No full explanation can be offered. While a more thorough study of the question will be necessary, several pertinent observations can be made.

Government involves the political enforcement of priorities. In newly developed countries, even more than in well-established lands, public services vary in the degree of attention that can be given to them. Almost everywhere, prisons rank low in priority among social welfare institutions. And they do in Israel.

No Jewish official had extensive experience in prison administration. Under British rule, Jews had been reluctant to enter a service that ranked low in its significance for the development of their national homeland. Only during the last few years of British rule had Jews entered the prison service in small numbers. Most of them were guards, assigned to prison work by the *Haganah,* the underground army. Their primary task was to protect Jewish political prisoners arrested in increasing numbers by the British authorities. The most able were concerned with such problems as how to sequester weapons and supplies from prison arsenals for use by the underground army. Prison work was a strategic assignment, not a chosen career.

The increase in criminal deviants and the need for prisons were unanticipated consequences of the most cherished objective of Jewish nationhood: the ingathering of exiles. The first law of the Jewish state, the *Law of Return,* entitles any person of the Jewish faith to enter Israel without a visa. The government can refuse entry only in cases of clearly identified state interest. There is little screening. The immigrants since 1948, therefore, include a higher ratio of deviants than existed among those who arrived earlier. Two out of three Israelis in 1962 had not been in the country when it became independent in 1948. Immigrants have streamed into the land, most of them without prior training and screening. All who could escape from Nazi-devastated Europe were welcome. Many were infirm, some were mentally ill, and a

2. The number of prison employees increased to 635 in December 1962, plus fourteen teachers and trade instructors provided by the Ministry of Labor and the Education authorities.

2

few were criminal. Nearly the entire Jewish communities of Iraq and Yemen were evacuated by air. The attainment of independence of Arab and North African countries was followed by a mass flight of Jews, including the poor and the deviants.

The Continuity of Administrative Structure

The legal system of the British mandatory government has left a lasting impact on the administration of justice in Israel. While the Jewish population objected to the mandatory government's use of authority, they admired its legal traditions. Many Israeli lawyers had British legal training. A model probation code, drafted in England but not adopted there because of Parliamentary opposition, was put in force in Palestine by order of the high commissioner. The criminal law in force in Palestine on May 14, 1948, was continued by the state of Israel. A major exception was the abolition of flogging as a legal form of punishment.

Israel also preserved the limitations of police power which had been introduced in Palestine under the British mandatory regime and even limited these powers further. As Edwin Samuel points out, they included among others the following procedures:

> No one can be arrested by the police in Israel without a magistrate warrant, unless caught in the act.
> No private home can be searched by the police without a warrant.
> Anyone arrested by the police must be charged within 48 hours with a specific offense.
> The *writ of habeas corpus* procedures can be employed by any lawyer who believes his client is being unlawfully detained.
> Accused persons with inadequate means are provided with competent legal counsel at government expense.
> There are adequate rights of appeal to higher courts against sentences in courts of first instance.[3]

During the British era, penal affairs were under the jurisdiction of three secretaries. A comparable division of function was continued in the new state. The administration of the Criminal Code Ordinances of 1936 and the ordinances governing the criminal procedure of courts were assigned to the Ministry of Justice. The Prison Ordinance of 1946 and the Police Ordinances became the jurisdiction of the Ministry of Police. The Probation Offender Ordinance of 1944 and the Juvenile Offender

3. Edwin Samuel, *Britain's Legacy to Israel*, The University of Leeds, The Fourth Selig Brodetsky Memorial Lecture, May 7, 1962, Leeds University Press, 1962, 9-10.

Ordinance of 1947 had been administered under British rule by a social welfare officer. The Israelis kept them in the same field, in the Ministry of Social Welfare. It has jurisdiction for adult and juvenile probation and for institutions for juvenile delinquents. As a result, several distinct and independent agencies are today related to the penal and penitentiary administration in Israel.

During the early years of the state, repeated questions were raised regarding the wisdom of this division of function.[4] The issue was solved on the basis of political rather than scientific considerations. The idea of unifying all law enforcement and penal agencies was advocated in the name of administrative efficiency. It was abandoned as politically impractical. None of the ministries which compose the country's coalition government wished to have its jurisdiction reduced. In an effort to coordinate their overlapping responsibilities, officials of the Ministry of Social Welfare were instrumental in establishing a National Council for the Prevention of Crime and Delinquency.[5]

The multijurisdictional structure of law enforcement agencies in Israel allows for the possibility of studying its administrative consequences. Many administrative specialists believe that it results in inefficiency. To what extent is this true? Is there encouragement of organizational competition that leads to innovation, under a system in which every administrator is considerably dependent on persons who can express their own point of view without being beholden to him for their career development? Our survey was too brief to answer these questions.

The continuity between the Israeli and the British traditions supports the conclusion that new social institutions do not develop after a revolution or independence, unless such change was a focus of the struggle. When Israel emerged, the government was converted from colonial office rule to parliamentary democracy. Jewish immigration, restricted under British rule, became unrestricted. But the structure of law enforcement processes was retained. In this low priority area of

4. Edmond Fitzgerald, *Report on a Six Week Study of Correctional Procedures in the State of Israel,* Tel Aviv: Government Printing Office, 1949, 10; see also Haim H. Cohn, "Introduction," *Treatment of Offenders in the State of Israel,* Tel Aviv: The Government Printer, July 1955. Cohn then was Attorney General of Israel.
5. The council is staffed by the legal counsellor of the Ministry, and includes officials from related government organizations and quasi-public voluntary organizations. The committee has no administrative power, but serves as a clearing house: (a) to facilitate more coordinated and effective approaches to the expenditure of funds related to crime and delinquency under the control of the respective organizations; (b) to reduce the tendency of persons in one organization to shift the blame for problems to those in other organizations; (c) to help people in the same field to become better acquainted; and (d) to appoint working sub-committees to make proposals for dealing with specific problems, to be submitted to the respective organizations or to the government.

government there was a gradual adaptive transition from mandatory policies.

When a new state is established, too much has to be done at once to give full attention to every one of the myriad functions of government. In Israel, as in most of the newly emerging countries of Asia and Africa, there had been no vacuum of law of tradition. The mandatory government had adapted many Ottoman laws in force when the British conquered Palestine in 1917. In fact, Israel today is one of the few countries of the world where Ottoman law survives as a significant component of family and real estate law.

Discontinuity in Philosophy

While the legal structure is essentially old — with modifications that increase each year — the system's spirit is new. A predominantly punitive approach has yielded to one that is primarily humanitarian. In Israel, as elsewhere, demands for stern measures and retribution will be heard whenever a heinous crime is committed. But these emotions are reacted to within a framework of compassion that has deep historical roots. During the Middle Ages, and in modern times, most Jews lived in ghettos. They have suffered the physical punishment and neglectful incarceration in vogue in most of the countries where they resided. Inside the ghettos deviants were usually dealt with by means of in-group extra-territorial social controls. There was great reluctance to call for punishment by the Gentile authorities.[6] Fines and in extreme cases banishment were favored sanctions. Repentance was encouraged. In Judaism spiritual grace attaches to the repentance of a sinner, as well as to his compassionate re-acceptance in the community.

This attitude of *Rachmanuth* (Hebrew for compassion) is reenforced by the reformist orientation of both socialism and Zionism. Socialism assumes that the ills of the lower classes (from which most criminals are derived) can be cured by sound economic measures. Zionism views Jewish statehood not as an end, but as a means for the attainment of a high moral order. Israel was not established only to serve the welfare of its citizens; it was established also to bring about the physical and spiritual redemption of Jewish minority groups all over the world, many of whom have lived under duress for centuries.

Many crimes occur under mitigating circumstances. Complex questions must be faced. How should one punish a thief or murderer who spent five years in a Nazi concentration camp, where he lost his entire

6. The writer had access to an unpublished study of the Jewish communal legal system during the Middle Ages, by Menachem Amir, Philadelphia, Pennsylvania: The University of Pennsylvania, 1962.

family in a gas oven? Or what is to be done with a Jew from Iran who killed his sister for having sexual relations outside of marriage, and thus compromising the family's honor? Is it criminal for an Arab youth to cross the border to try life among his relatives though he violates state security regulations in the process? Israel has energetic law-enforcement agencies, but sentences of convicted criminals tend to be compassionate. Prison is resorted to with reluctance, particularly for first offenders.

The development of penal policy has also been affected by the fact that many citizens have experienced the role of outcast. Israel probably has the highest concentration of population in the world of persons who have been imprisoned for religious or political reasons. The old-time Israelis (those living in the country before 1948) had been imprisoned or had intimately known persons imprisoned by the Turks or British for resistance to regulations the Jewish population regarded as inconsistent with the goal that a Jewish national home be established in Palestine. Many had experienced incarceration in Nazi concentration camps before or during World War II. Others had served time in Russian, Rumanian and other "old country" prisons because as Jews, Socialists or liberals they were defined as being a danger to the government.

In Israel the death penalty for murder has been abolished. It is restricted to cases of treason and genocide. Life is held in high esteem. The antipathy toward the death penalty was fed by a tragic circumstance during the first days of Israel's war of liberation. A Jewish employee of the Jerusalem Electric Company was summarily tried for treason by a field court martial and executed. Subsequent investigation showed that he was innocent. No statements of regret by the Prime Minister and posthumous restoration of his civil rights could bring him back to life. Since then, all death sentences have been commuted by the President, with the exception of that for Adolf Eichmann who was convicted for his leadership in the genocide of over six million Jews, plus millions of other Europeans.

No Arab spies or saboteurs (and many have been caught) have been placed before a firing squad, in spite of contrary practices in Arab states across the border. Infiltrators and saboteurs are tried by the courts. Upon conviction they are imprisoned in the same institutions and under the same circumstances as Israeli criminals. After serving their sentences — usually only two-thirds of the time originally imposed — they are quietly returned to the countries of their origin through the mixed armistice commissions of Israel with Egypt, Jordan, Syria and Lebanon.

The imposition of legal sanctions against criminals is characterized by humanitarianism. While there is no evidence that such mercy prevents or deters crime, it is advocated for its own sake. Humanism in Israel's

6

penal policy reflects not only compassion for the offender, but it expresses a value that is deeply rooted in the society that sits in judgment.

Legal Reforms

From the beginning of statehood Israel has dealt with mental patients and drug addicts outside penal institutions. Persons who are clearly mentally ill are sent to mental hospitals. Drug addicts (not drug smugglers or "pushers") are put under medical supervision. Young prostitutes are sent to treatment-oriented institutions. All juvenile delinquents are under the jurisdiction of the social- work-oriented Ministry of Social Welfare.

A reform emphasis is also characteristic of the management of adult criminals. In 1954, a series of legal changes was introduced to modify Israeli law enforcement practices. Among the procedural changes that were adopted were the following:

1. Courts are authorized to substitute suspended sentences for imprisonment.

2. Punishments provided by law are deemed to be maximum, and courts can reduce penalties if they so desire. When imprisonment is imposed on the same offender for several offenses, the imprisonment is to run concurrently unless the court orders the sentences or part of them to be cumulative.

3. Imprisonment for periods exceeding one year can be imposed only after report on the accused has been submitted by a probation officer.[7]

4. Token wage payments to prisoners doing productive work are authorized.

5. Visiting and correspondence privileges have been liberalized.

6. Persons who have been accused of a law violation can be awarded costs for their defense if the complaint is found groundless. Conversely, upon conviction the accused may be ordered to bear the cost of prosecution, in addition to any punishment imposed.

7. A Release Board was set up to review all sentences of imprison-

7. This regulation carries out one of the recommendations of Edmond Fitzgerald, chief probation officer of Brooklyn, New York, who served as a consultant to the Israeli government in 1949 (*Report on a Six Week Study of Correctional Procedures in the State of Israel,* Tel Aviv, Israel: Government Printer, 1949). The Minister of Justice delayed the implementation of this rule until 1962. While he was urged to act by the Ministry of Social Welfare, the Ministry of Finance requested this delay. There was not enough money to hire the additional probation officers, even for a limited implementation of the regulation for youths between sixteen and twenty-one. When this regulation was finally put into force, the work of the adult probation department increased by 100 per cent, whereas their staff could be increased by only 40 per cent. The impact of this discrepancy on the quality of the work performed was not investigated.

ment of more than six months. After two-thirds of the sentence has been served, the remainder can be remitted by the action of the board composed of a district judge, the commissioner of prisons or his representative and a physician or educator. Earlier releases can be ordered in exceptional cases — such as severe chronic illness. The Minister of Police on his own discretion can order the release of persons sentenced for short terms, for three to six months. He can decide these cases without the advice of the Release Board, but he generally acts only on a recommendation of the prison administration.

The structure of the law in Israel has changed slowly since its independence. But the spirit of its implementation has changed markedly. Prominent individuals have publicly criticized the leniency of the courts in specific cases. But with apparent support of important segments of public opinion, judges show much compassion for ameliorating circumstances in offenses that come before them for adjudication. Legal procedures have been changed to facilitate the systematic application of humanitarian ideas in the way convicted criminals are dealt with by the state. In Biblical times, the principle "an eye for an eye" was enunciated as a reform of the previously favored practice of imposing the death penalty for many offenses. But today it is completely out of date in its country of origin. The criminal, rather than his crime, is given strong consideration in deciding what punishment is to be imposed.

The Ascendancy of Science

The sciences enjoy high esteem in Israel. The country's first President, and a dominant political figure for over three decades before the establishment of the state, was the renowned chemist Dr. Chaim Weizmann.[8] Its second President, Yitchak Ben Zvi, published a definitive work on the sociological history and customs of diverse oriental Jewish ethnic communities.[9] These symbolic figures are backed up by a substantive diffusion of scientific accomplishments throughout the entire country. Israel has become a refuge for Jewish scientists persecuted or handicapped in many lands, and it probably holds the world record in density of scientists and the volume of scholarly books published and sold. There are five institutions of higher learning. Scientific experts are being "exported" to render aid to other newly emerging countries.

A scientific outlook was also reflected in an early awareness by the

8. He was director of British Admiralty laboratories during most of World War I and instrumental in the discovery of technical processes that contributed much to Britain's victory. He founded the Weizmann Institute of Science, the country's principal basic research facility in the physical and biological sciences.
9. *The Exiled and the Redeemed,* Philadelphia: Jewish Publication Society of America, 1957.

Israeli government that it lacked the basis for a sound penal policy. Within less than a year of its establishment, the Ministry of Justice invited Edmond Fitzgerald, chief probation officer of the Brooklyn County Court, to make a survey of correctional procedures.[10] Israel welcomed several United Nations experts and participated in the first and second United Nations Congresses on the Prevention of Crime and the Treatment of Offenders, held in 1955 and 1960. Reports on Israel's penal system were prepared for both occasions.

In 1956 a United Nations survey of criminological services in Israel resulted in the establishment of the Institute of Criminology at the Hebrew University in Jerusalem. As is evident from the references used in this report, several criminological studies have been made that have a bearing on critical prison management problems. An undergraduate training program in criminology has been established at Bar-Ilan University near Tel Aviv. The prison system employs two social scientists to work with its own scientific director on the improvement of fact-gathering procedures. Other research resources are found in the department of sociology at the Hebrew University and the Israeli Institute for Applied Social Research — the country's principal survey research center. The Society for the Rehabilitation of Prisoners actively lobbies for penal reform and other help to selected prisoners after their release.

Israeli criminologists are dissatisfied with the use of these resources for the applications of science to policy-making. In the prison system, there has been much improvisation. In the agricultural, technological and medical fields, the latest scientific discoveries are rapidly applied. In the prisons, there is far more promise than fulfilment. Avowed aspirations for scientific achievement exceed resources for their attainment.

This discrepancy will be elaborated in more detail. It is not a condition peculiar to Israel. It is world wide. In Israel, as elsewhere, there is concern with the fact that many fundamental penological questions remain unsolved. Prison administrators know that they face essentially the same questions posed by Signor Scalia in 1870 at the first American Prison Congress when he reviewed conditions from 1820 to his time:

For the last fifty years, the efficiency of the different penitentiary systems has been carefully debated, but that question has not yet made much progress; and, at present, as was the case a long time ago, the champions of different schools are ranged in the field of abstractions, to go over the same arguments, and to allege on both sides the same facts and experiments. Though chains have been broken, though corporal punishment has been abolished, though the prisoner receives a better treatment than heretofore, though indulgence and leniency have now superseded the severity of punishment, nobody can tell me whether and how far this humanitarian spirit has stopped the corrupting current of guilt; what have been the effects of . . . [certain punishments]; and none can inform me why they have deemed it better to be more

10. Edmond Fitzgerald, *op. cit.*

9

lenient or more severe, and the problem about relapse still remains unsolved.[11]

Scalia's summary of the state of criminological knowledge remains as up to date in 1963 as it was in 1870. The contrast between the rate of scientific discovery and the rate of application is probably more keenly felt in Israel than in some other modern countries, because of the general commitment of many of its citizens to the application of intelligence to the solution of complex human problems. Israel is a land that has been appropriately caricatured as not just a sociological melting pot but as a "pressure cooker." Government is conducted with an expectation that a high degree of perfection will be obtained.

Prisons in Utopia

Ever since Roman legions put an end to the second Jewish state in the year 70 A.D., Jews have vowed in prayer, "If I forget you, O Jerusalem, let my right hand wither!" Palestine was the locus of an ethnic-religious Utopia. In 1896, the founder of political Zionism, Dr. Theodor Herzl, called on Jews not to wait until a Messiah would return them miraculously to their historic patrimony. He called for political action and an active settlement policy to accomplish this goal. In 1948, the state of Israel was a reality.[12]

Modern Israel was founded on more than mere nationalism. It aimed to do more than return the Jews to Palestine, where they could live under a government free from anti-Semitism. Zionism had as a primary objective the reform of the individual Jew through a planned environmental change. Men would be remade by living in a planned social system dominated by leaders with high ethical concern, technological productivity, personal courage — and within an atmosphere of freedom and social justice. The Jewish effort to build a national home was seen as a contribution to bring about a better world. The movement embraced aspirations for a realistic Utopia that could inspire humanity just as Israel had once given birth to the Bible. In 1902, Herzl wrote about the country he aspired to create, in his novel *Alt-Neuland*.[13] He saw it governed by an elite of idealists, but there also was room for average mortals, even for criminals.

11. Martino Beltrani Scalia, "Historical Sketch of National and International Penitentiary Conferences in Europe and America," New York Prison Association, *Twenty-sixth Annual Report*, 1871.
12. The idea of a Jewish national revival in Palestine gave rise to a series of proposals and movements, especially during the Middle Ages and Renaissance. In 1878, the first Jewish agricultural settlement was established, eighteen years before Herzl made his proposals for political and economic action that gave rise to a mass movement. (Rufus Learsi, *Fulfillment*, Cleveland and New York: The World Publishing Co., 1951, 1-5.)
13. Theodor Herzl, *Alt-Neuland*, Haifa, Israel: Haifa Publishing Co., 1960.

10

Herzl envisioned the country's prison as a model farm, a minimum custody institution where men would be taught to work. In answer to the question, "And how effective is the process of rehabilitation?" he predicted that most inmates would be reformed. He described the prison as a place where "people regained their physical and moral health. A great many become fond of country life, and after they have done their stretch, start out as paid laborers, to be settled after a while on farms in outlying districts." Herzl concluded his description of the Alt-Neuland with a hopeful observation: "We can truly say that our system makes men again of the scum of mankind." [14]

Herzl had introduced his Utopian novel with the admonition to fellow Jews: *"If you will, it is no fairy-tale."* Sixty-two years later, many of his aspirations have become reality.[15] Others have exceeded the wildest expectations of this dreamer. But, as he had perceived, there have also been people with human frailties. Prisons have been needed.

When police Colonel Gero Geyra was appointed acting director of prisons in 1948, he had to scrounge for supplies to clean the old British prisons for use, until it was possible to convert the abandoned police barracks at Tel Mond into a more modern prison. The foundation of the new prison system was not planned; it was improvised. Israel was besieged on all borders by its Arab neighbors who had rejected the United Nations resolution that had given the state its legal status. A sizable part of Israel's national income was (and still is) spent on national defense.

An even larger part of the budget is devoted to taking care of the inrush of immigrants who stream into the land of their Biblical fathers. Most immigrants arrive with nothing but handbaggage. It is all that they can salvage from such lands as Iraq, Egypt, Poland and Yemen, where they and many generations of forebears lived. New housing, bedding and every kitchen pot have to be provided. Ten thousands of children have arrived without parents. And there are many aged and infirm.

The care and treatment of prisoners — people who stand aside from this great effort at human redemption — can hardly count on a high priority under such circumstances. The appearance of a criminal problem of sufficient size to require public attention is ideologically distasteful. It implies doubts about the validity of the theory that a national and social renaissance will cure all individual ills.

14. *Ibid.,* 177.
15. Zionism is a dramatic illustration of the validity of the Thomas theorem, or what Robert K. Merton has called the "self-fulfilling prophecy." It refers to the fact that what men believe to be true, or possible of attainment, influences them to behave in a manner to make realization of their hopes more likely. Robert K. Merton, *Social Theory and Social Structure,* New York: The Free Press of Glencoe, 1957, 421-436.

At first, the new prison service had no budget of its own. Funds had to be diverted from the budget of the Ministry of Police, also in its formative period. Even after the prison department was made administratively autonomous on January 1, 1949, costly programs could not be considered — there could be no new buildings, no professionally trained staff, no extensive inmate treatment programs. Within the limits of manpower that could be borrowed or co-opted in 1949, work programs were introduced.

The acting director, who retired in 1952, was replaced by a commissioner, Dr. Zvi Hermon, who served in that capacity until 1958. During his six years of executive responsibility, the basic policy was: Humanitarianism is necessary, but not sufficient. The prison service also needs the application of scientific principles in order to maximize its capability of reforming the inmates.

Work and treatment programs were expanded. In 1952 the only treatment person in the prison system was a physician. Gradually, funds were obtained to employ twenty-one social workers, three general practitioners, two psychiatrists and a part-time psychologist. Legislatively and administratively the spirit of innovation rode high, as it did in other of the country's public services; but there were budgetary limits to the full-fledged professionalization of the penal system. Edmond Fitzgerald reported that when he arrived in Israel in 1949 as a consultant on correctional procedures, the Minister of Justice and the Attorney General told him to keep in mind "the economic condition of the new nation and its need to put first things first." [16] And prison work was not viewed as a high priority field. Funds and personnel were always in short supply, and the need to care for prisoners grew. But Fitzgerald found that in the law enforcement field, "as with every aspect of life and activity in this progressive young nation, the physical limitations are compensated for by the high caliber of the personnel who have to deal with them and surmount them. Everywhere there is the most remarkable improvisation. Everywhere the accent is on the human equation."

Unattained Aspirations

The prison commissioner, as well as leading political figures, was knowledgeable about the traditions and penal practices of Russia, Germany, England, France, Turkey, the United States, Mexico and many other countries. In the history of human affairs, the opportunity is rare to set up penal institutions on the basis of deliberate choice from alternative patterns. Such an opportunity existed in Israel when its prison

16. Edmond Fitzgerald, op. cit.

12

system was organized. Those responsible for the task were conscious of it, and their aspirations were not satisfied with meeting minimum or modest standards of performance.

In the beginning, improvisation was a necessity. Israel had no cadre of professional criminologists. Prison facilities had to be set up for a population larger than had been expected. These limitations were not allowed to become a permanent fixture. There were gradual improvements. In 1957 Dr. Israel Drapkin summarized prison conditions as follows in a United Nations survey of Israel's criminological services:

Generally it can be said that Israeli prisons are functioning to a certain extent in accordance with the "Minimum Rules for the Treatment of Prisoners" adopted by the First United Nations Congress on the Prevention of Crime and the Treatment of Offenders, held in Geneva in 1955. In fact the prisons are located away from the densely populated urban areas; although the inmates are housed in old buildings, the rooms in the majority of cases are large and airy. There is still room for further improvement. In most cases although still short of specialized staff, prisoners receive medical and psychiatric care and also social services are available to them. Workshops, vocational training units and "hobby" shops are in operation and provide for paid work; instruction in several crafts and "hobby" activities; agricultural work on a wide scale is also a very practical reality; food is varied, healthy and sufficient; education, cultural and leisure time programmes are very intensive; the inmates participate in some aspects of the administration sitting together with prison officers in several committees, like those dealing with the reception of new inmates, problems of work and vocational training, welfare and cultural activities, sports, food control, and others, etc. But what is still more important is the absence of constraint and the lack of an antagonistic atmosphere. This prevents among prisoners states of anxiety or frustration. Thus the ground is prepared for the rehabilitation of prisoners through constructive work.[17]

Israel came into being because its supporters believed that what is difficult can be achieved; the impossible takes just a little longer. As one views developments since 1948, it becomes apparent that this outlook has a pervasive influence on the way general policy is being translated into day-to-day operations. Innovations are favored, within a limiting condition characteristic of most large administrative systems whose officials yearn for a stable structure, to maximize predictability and to enhance security conditions.

17. Israel Drapkin, *Criminological Services in Israel,* New York: United Nations, Report No. TAA/ISR/23, October 1, 1957: 5. Dr. Drapkin was subsequently appointed head of the Institute of Criminology at the Hebrew University.

The Prison System

The British prisons were located in medieval buildings with insufficient light and fresh air. Those at Acre and Jerusalem were never reopened. Fourteen young men had been hanged there, with their lives before them, for what the British had regarded as terrorist acts. To Jews they were heroes of the struggle for independence, personally known to many in the land. It seemed in bad taste to use these same British prisons to quarter common criminals. The Jerusalem installation was turned into a storage area for educational books, and the historic crusader fortress at Acre, made well known through the novel *Exodus,* was converted into a mental hospital.

Improvised Installations

There was neither time nor priority to allocate enough money to build prisons. Four of the country's six new prisons are converted Teggart police fortresses, built in the 1930's by the British at strategic points throughout Palestine to control the country. In addition to thick walls and small windows with bars, these fortresses had apartments for police officers and their families that could be converted into offices and into dormitories for inmates. Small farms and workshops were attached to the main buildings. Barbed wire fences, originally built by the British to protect those within, were kept and reenforced to keep inmates from breaking out.

Food, clothing and bedding in prisons are provided at standards equal to those of the armed forces, whose quartermaster's corps has a contract to procure food for all penal installations. Since 1956 all prisoners sentenced for more than three months are first sent to an observation and classification center at Tel Mond. Ramle Prison has a central hospital and dental clinic as well as a psychiatric department for mentally unbalanced prisoners. Those who are clearly psychotic are transferred to a mental hospital. Separate maximum security quarters for dangerous inmates are maintained, as well as a detention department for persons who are being held for trial.[1]

1. The following prisons were in existence in 1962: Ramle Prison, the country's maximum security facility — a converted police fortress; Tel Mond Prison, a close security facility and classification center (it is a converted police fortress with an adjoining minimum-custody camp for 28 youthful offenders); Damoun Prison and Shatta Prison, housing both Jewish and Arab prisoners under close security conditions; Neve Tirza, a small close security facility for women, also a former police fortress; and Massiyahu Camp, for more trusted inmates, a minimum-custody facility. Police lock-ups are located in major cities, including Tel Aviv-Jaffa, Jerusalem, Haifa, Beer Sheba and Nazareth. They are used only to keep individuals for short periods, after their arrest or during court trials. Persons arrested and detained for more than a few days are sent to a prison.

14

The prison system maintains twenty-three work units, directed by an officer. Inmates are paid modest wages. In addition, the Ministry of Labor operates twelve trade courses which are taught by civilian specialists who also arrange for supplementary theoretical lectures and visits by the inmates to factories outside the prisons. Successful participants receive a certificate entitling them, upon release, to apply for membership in the appropriate trade union. The prison is not named as the training location.[2]

Most of the inmates who are well and employable are occupied with work programs. They produce clothes, shoes and other items for the prisons and various governmental units. Flowers for export are produced at Massiyahu. About half of the inmates are trained in workshops to earn a livelihood upon release. Many others are ineligible because their sentences are too brief to complete a trade course. This is one reason why many officials question the country's short sentence policy. Such short-termers are more likely to be put to work in prison maintenance units, food preparation, laundry, cleaning and other establishments.

Small Installations

What happens to inmates in a prison depends only in part on the policies and programs conducted there. Also important, and often missed, is the operational impact of location and organizational size. The fact that most inmates in Israel's prisons are housed in converted police barracks has had the consequence, in the view of the department's scientific director, of making "it difficult always to guarantee maximum security without imposing the kind of discipline which creates an atmosphere antagonistic to endeavors aiming at the correction and rehabilitation of offenders."[3] But an observer to whom the word prison is associated with large prison cities like San Quentin, which houses over 4,600 felons, finds the prisons of Israel to be relatively informal institutions.

Even the largest installation at Ramle, with a capacity of approximately four hundred, has many attributes of a small community. The prison director can have personal knowledge of every one of his staff. He can know most of the inmates, certainly those who remain in the institution for any length of time, and if an inmate is sick he is not simply a body in a hospital bed. Ramle has no long lines of men patiently waiting to be let into the dining room. Anonymity and social distance that are necessary attributes of every large-scale organization do not seem to

2. For a detailed recent description of the prison administration see Zvi Hermon, "Correctional Progress in Israel, 1948-61," *American Journal of Corrections*, Vol. 25, No. 2, 1963, 4-18.
3. *Ibid.*, 9. This comment applies particularly to Ramle, the country's largest prison. It is much less true of Tel Mond, Massiyahu and Neve Tirza.

be pronounced in any of the six small installations that comprise the Israeli prison system.

American prison sub-cultures subjected to intensive study were those of large-scale, highly impersonal total institutions.[4] The writer suspects that the character of the Israeli inmate culture is different. Most prisoners have short sentences. Convicts who are deeply identified with criminal mores are uncommon. Certainly in theory, the capacity of the staff to influence the inmate social system is greatly enhanced under such conditions.

For selected purposes, outsiders are encouraged to have social interactions with inmates. In 1962 a group of students at Tel Aviv University "adopted" Tel Mond Reformatory. They teach classes there. The inmates have a dramatic group, which performs publicly. It was hampered in its choice of plays because the performers were all men. This problem was solved in 1963 when girl students from Tel Aviv University volunteered to take female roles in *Monsemat* by Robles. The girls had to travel for rehearsals to Tel Mond over a period of four months.[5]

Damoun

Illustrative of Israel's prisons is Damoun, located on wooded Mt. Carmel. It has one of Israel's most scenic locations, overlooking the Mediterranean. This prison is twenty minutes from the city of Haifa, in a former tobacco curing plant. In April 1962 it housed 113 Jewish and 138 Arab inmates. Damoun also has a mixed cadre of Jewish and Arab prison guards. Inmates, particularly youthful prisoners from the north, are sent from Tel Mond Classification Center, an hour's ride away. Damoun has two wings, a newly built dormitory wing and a reconditioned wing containing rooms of the former farm buildings. The latter are reserved for prisoners of model behavior who can have more privacy. There are basketball and volley ball courts, a recreation room and a modest library. Some of the cells, however, have "only a narrow aperture for light and a bucket for sanitary needs." [6] Inmates are often kept in these cells from the early hours of the evening until morning.

When a prisoner is admitted, he passes through three locked gates, each guarded by an unarmed officer. The inmate is first taken into a supply room, where he is asked to undress within a blanket cubicle.

4. Donald Clemmer, *The Prison Community*, Boston: The Christopher Publishing House, 1940; Gresham M. Sykes, *The Society of Captives*, Princeton: The Princeton University Press, 1958; and Donald R. Cressey, ed., *The Prison: Studies in Institutional Organization and Change*, New York: Holt, Rinehart and Winston, 1961.

5. *The Israel Digest*, Vol. VI, No. 4, February 15, 1963, 5.

6. Report by Supreme Court Justice Berinson, Chairman of the Society for the Rehabilitation of Prisoners, *Jerusalem Post*, Friday, January 18, 1963: II.

Personal belongings and valuables that have been returned to him for safekeeping before his transfer from Tel Mond prison are once again taken away. They are stored after a receipt is issued. Each prisoner is then medically examined and given prison clothes. His own garments are put into storage. Every six months he can have them washed, cleaned and hung up, to be ready for the day of discharge.

After this admissions procedure, prisoners are taken through the prison. But there is not much to see. The entire compound, including a farm area, covers about ten acres. Prison rules are explained and each inmate is assigned to one of the dormitory rooms.

Damoun places much emphasis on training. Illiterates are taught to read and write. Agriculture, building trades, and laundry and kitchen work keep some of the inmates busy. Civilian instructors, paid by the Ministry of Labor, conduct apprenticeship courses in carpentry, printing, bookbinding, tailoring and shoemaking. The instructors wear no uniforms. Their technical supervisors are vocational educators, not prison officials.

Three isolation cells are occasionally used for disciplinary purposes. More often they are inhabited by older or long-term inmates who, as a reward for good behavior, are offered a little more privacy. All other inmates sleep in dormitory rooms, which are under guard. On good behavior, selected inmates can advance into a special privilege dormitory. It is neither locked nor under constant guard. No inmate is assigned without a favorable vote of the group. Its members have to be responsible for self-discipline.

About once a week a basketball team from the neighboring Jewish village of Bet Oren or the Druse village of Issfiyah is brought to the prison for a game. On occasions, the inmates may be taken to these villages to play there.

The prison has a doctor and two full-time and one half-time social workers. Two of them are women who have their offices in the prison. The half-time worker, a man, helps inmates about to be released to Haifa in their arrangements for release.

The physical facilities, food and medical care of Damoun compare favorably with those available to lower class inmates in their outside lives. One Arab youth from Gaza, under Egyptian control, crossed the border into Israel a second time and explained, upon apprehension, that he had returned to have his dental work completed! Planned programs exist to contribute to the rehabilitation capability of each inmate.

The professionals employed by the prison system, while taking pride in what has been accomplished, express concern over the insufficiency of social service manpower. Intensive counselling cannot be offered to more than a handful. There is uncertainty about the relationship of the work training program to the opportunity structure of many of the inmates. Prison employees, especially the guards, have insufficient training to deal with the complex social and psychological demands made upon anyone who is responsible for the management of prisoners.

The Israeli prisons rank high by comparison with facilities in all of the neighboring countries. They are comparable to older jails and prisons in technologically advanced countries like the United States and Great Britain. But the national ethos of Israel is supportive of higher standards. A visiting committee of Israel's Society for the Rehabilitation of Prisoners denounced Damoun and Shatta for being overcrowded and demanded that conditions be improved.[7]

Criminal Deviancy

Criminal offenses among Jews were rare before the establishment of Israel. Nevertheless, before independence was achieved, the country had many prisons and detention camps. Most of the Jewish and some of the Arab inmates were political offenders. They had violated laws or taken to arms in the cause of their respective national objectives. Over 24,000 future Jewish citizens were interned on the island of Cyprus for trying to enter Palestine illegally. The majority of Israel's first cabinet had a prison record. In the office of Aryeh Nir, the commissioner of prisons, is a photograph of himself in prison garb. While employed as a police officer by the mandatory government, he was apprehended with a truck full of explosives during a night when most of Palestine's bridges to Arab countries were blown up by the Jewish underground army as a defense measure. For this felony he was convicted and sentenced to prison.

The independence of Israel, followed, as it was, by the mass immigration of Jews from all over the world, meant the beginning of new problems. Before World War II, and especially before 1933, Israel attracted immigrants who came from relatively secure backgrounds, from families who had middle-class status. They were revolting against anti-Semitism and the limited opportunity structure for personal and communal development. They were mostly nationalistic, socialistic and Utopian. Their personal goals were subordinated to social objectives.

After the establishment of the state, only a small proportion of the immigrants came from such idealistic middle- and upper-class families. Fewer immigrants were strongly identified with pioneering objectives.

7. *Jerusalem Post, ibid.* As a result of this criticism, the Police Minister granted the society's request to inspect prisons without advance notice.

Many were underprivileged and uneducated, and some were criminals.[8] Recorded offenses rose from nearly 17,000 in 1949 to over 56,000 in 1960.[9] The net increase in recorded offenses was less spectacular. But it nearly doubled, from 1,446 in 1949 to 2,611 per 100,000 population in 1960.

Reasons for this increase cannot be investigated in this study. There are crimes by and convictions of older residents, but the bulk of the increase of antisocial behavior is accounted for by the unselected influx of immigrants after 1949 who came from approximately seventy different countries. Many of the immigrants had experienced traumatic and disorganizing experiences such as loss of family members by persecution, loss of property, and loss of social status. More than half of the new citizens came from economically underdeveloped and culturally premodern Middle Eastern lands, including Yemen, Iraq, Morocco and Tunis. Israeli observers agreed with E. Millo that "immigration and the process of integration of newcomers in such large numbers have led to [the] disorganization of patterns of life traditional to the immigrants, and the impact of this has in turn led to much maladjustment and delinquency among their youth." [10] In a sociological survey, Professor R. Bachi of the Hebrew University has shown that Jewish children from Oriental countries leave school at an early age and have a high percentage of absenteeism and backwardness. These Oriental immigrant groups have a low percentage of children in school.[11] Similar disorganization trends exist among the adults.

In Israel, as in most lands, the probability of being caught may be somewhat higher for lower-class persons than for the more established settlers. Deviations in the *Kibbutzim* (collective villages) and the army are probably underreported because they are often handled by means of informal controls, without resort to the police. In the cities, however, persons from "good" families, especially children, are found in disturbing-

8. S. N. Eisenstadt, *The Absorption of Immigrants: A Comparative Study Based Mainly on the Jewish Community in Palestine and the State of Israel,* London: Routledge & Kegan Paul Ltd., 1954, 27-45.

9. Juvenile offenders are excluded from this survey. In 1958, the juvenile courts handled 836 cases, about 8 boys for every girl offender. At the end of the year, 575 children were committed to care outside their homes — in governmental welfare institutions, private schools or foster homes. In addition, 384 children were released from such facilities during the year. Most juvenile problems are handled by the Youth Probation Service without a formal court conviction. In 1958, a total of 6,327 investigations were made and 1,148 youngsters had been placed on probation.

10. E. Millo, *Prevention of Types of Criminality Resulting from Social Changes and Accompanying Economic Development in Less Developed Countries,* Jerusalem, Israel: Ministry of Social Welfare, Division of Research and Planning, May 1960, 1.

11. Quoted by S. N. Eisenstadt, "The Oriental Jew in Israel," New York: *Jewish Social Studies,* Vol. XII, No. 3, 212.

TABLE 1*

Volume of Recorded Offenses and Prison Population in Israel — 1949-1960

Year	Number of Recorded Offenses	Total No. Received in Years for Detention or Conviction	Yearly Average No. of Prison Inmates Detained and Convicted	Total Population at End of Year**	Rates per 100,000 Population	
					Recorded Offenses	Yearly Average Inmates Detained and Convicted
1949	16,982		181	1,173,871	1,446	15
1950	22,062	NOT	409	1,370,094	1,610	29
1951	33,554		598	1,577,825	2,126	37
1952	37,934	GIVEN	842	1,629,519	2,327	51
1953	35,371		1,092	1,669,417	2,118	65
1954	36,940		1,034	1,717,814	2,150	60
1955	36,734	3,102	923	1,789,075	2,053	51
1956	43,718	2,677	890	1,872,390	2,334	47
1957	46,259	3,196	990	1,975,954	2,341	50
1958	48,320	3,639	1,091	2,031,672	2,378	53
1959	49,609	3,636	?	2,088,685	2,375	?
1960	56,146	3,734	1,091†	2,150,412	2,611	41†

* Adapted from O. Schmelz and D. Salzman, *Criminal Statistics in Israel*, 1949-1958, Jerusalem. Publication of the Institute of Criminology, The Hebrew University, Jerusalem, 1962. Tables 1, 90 and 91. Information for 1959 and 1960 provided by the prison service.
** From Statistical Bulletin of Israel, dated August 1961, Part 1, page 325.
† Based on the number of inmates on the last day of 1960.

ly large numbers among those who are brought to court. This fact gives rise to concern that the new generation will not live up to the standards of the present generation.

Fewer than one-third of the recorded offenses result in a conviction. For 44 per cent of the 48,320 recorded crimes in 1958, no suspect could be identified. Over 13 per cent of the complaint files were closed after investigation, and no action was taken.[12] Many other charges were dismissed by a court, the accused were acquitted, or they died. But 14,094 adults were convicted for serious offenses, including affrays and minor assaults.[13]

Israeli judges are sparing in their use of imprisonment for convicted offenders. Only about one in four convicted criminals ever sees the inside of a prison. The proportion of persons incarcerated in Israel is certainly smaller than in the United States as a whole or in the state of California alone. During 1960 an average of only 41 per 100,000 Israelis were imprisoned at any one time.[14] Throughout that year, 3,734 persons had been sent to prison, but most of them had short sentences. Some were detained only for investigation, since Israel's jails are not generally used to hold suspects for more than a day or two.

For many old settlers, the existence of a sizable criminal population in Israel was a surprise. The idealists who pioneered the country's absorptive resources for immigrants were disappointed and dismayed; they had risked their lives to bring refugees into the country. Although criminal deviations were unacceptable, the Israelis understood that immigration, especially from Near Eastern countries, required a difficult transition.[15] Many old values were in conflict with those of the new society. For instance, the use of personal violence to settle personal complaints or to protect the "family honor" was more acceptable in non-Western than in Western cultures.

The police are vigilant in investigating crimes. The office of the

12. O. Schmelz and D. Salzman, *Criminal Statistics in Israel,* 1949-1958, Jerusalem, Israel: Publications of the Institute of Criminology, No. 1, the Hebrew University, 1962, Tables 107, 110, 216, 219.

13. Offenses recorded in the charge register of the police, a detailed form about the offense, the offender and the outcome of the trial.

14. Rates of Imprisonment in Israel and the United States per 100,000:
   Israel (1960) 41*
   U.S.A. (Excluding Alaska, 1960) 120**
   California (1960) 134

 * Israel has limited jail facilities. This rate includes large numbers of short-term cases, sentenced to less than a year and persons detained only for investigation. Some of them are not convicted.
** Largely felony convictions of more than a year. These rates do *not* include persons serving jail sentences or held for investigation, as is the case with the Israeli rates. If jail rates were included, the American totals would be much higher.

15. David Reifen, *The Juvenile Court in Israel,* Jerusalem: Ministry of Justice, 1962, 15.

Attorney General will prosecute if the evidence warrants prosecution. But once a conviction is obtained, and the culprit is degraded thereby, there is a pronounced preference for restoration of his social status through reformation.

Change in the Nature of Deviancy

The definition of a criminal security offense changed when the British high commissioner's departure on a warship in Haifa Bay signaled the end of the League of Nations' mandate over Palestine. Stealing government property, bribing public officials, smuggling and using force for patriotic purposes were part of the prelude to independence in Israel, as they have been in almost every national battle for liberation. Such acts were often committed by idealists, at great personal risk. But once independence was achieved, these very same acts became criminal, a serious threat to the new government.

The British had tolerated many Arab efforts to oppose Jewish settlement as a legitimate expression of their national self-interest. The state of Israel could not take so neutral an approach if it wanted to survive. Governments associated with the Arab League declared open warfare the moment Israel's establishment was voted by the United Nations.

On the order of their leaders, many Arab inhabitants of Palestine left their homes to give Arab armies a free hand in the invasion of areas where the Jewish and Arab population had been living in proximity. Others fled in fear of Jewish reprisals for the activities of Arab guerilla forces. All of them expected to return within a few weeks, after the Jewish state had been wiped out.

When these military calculations failed the Arabs became refugees. After Israel's borders were established through armistice agreements with neighboring Arab states, the Arabs remaining in Israel became a minority. Many have accepted this reality, but some have not. Espionage and sabotage have been actively promoted by Israel's neighbors even after the signing of armistice agreements, and continuous efforts are made to elicit the cooperation of the Arab citizens of Israel.[16] The government aims to counteract this propaganda by a combination of positive and security measures. Much is being done to improve the life of Arab citizens; they enjoy the highest standard of living of any Arab population

16. For instance between September 1961 and March 1962 eleven Israeli Arabs who had previously fled to Gaza in Egypt were returned by the Egyptian intelligence to Israel. The statistics obviously include only those who were caught by Israeli security forces. The stories which they had to tell the Israeli authorities were all of a similar pattern. They left home because of private quarrels or legal involvements rather than a deliberate attempt to join the Egyptian forces in Gaza. But once they arrived there, they were forced to work for the Egyptian intelligence. (From a news story in the *Jerusalem Post*, Tuesday, April 17, 1962.)

22

group in the Middle East. But there are divisions of loyalty that create a security problem of major proportions. In the words of Prime Minister David Ben-Gurion:

The Proclamation of Independence declared: "The State of Israel will maintain complete equality of social and political rights for all its citizens, without distinction of creed, race or sex." Accordingly, for instance, Arab women have been given equal status with the men: polygamy is forbidden for Jews and Arabs alike. The siege which Egypt, Jordan, Syria and Lebanon set upon Israel, the avowed policy of their rulers to destroy Israel, obliged and still oblige the State to adopt special security precautions in the border areas, which are under military administration. In this situation, Israel's Arab citizens are exempt from the civic duty of military service. The Druzes and Circassians are an exception: at first they joined up voluntarily, but in 1956, at the instance of their communal leaders, the men — not the women — were made liable to conscription; there are also some Arab Christian volunteers. Otherwise, full equality of rights and duties is guaranteed to all Israelis, without distinction of creed or nationality . . . .[17]

Israelis who violate security regulations or citizens of neighboring states who cross Israel's borders as saboteurs and marauders are usually sent to prison. Their offenses are serious. Often they take the form of killing or maiming and of destroying property. The major deterrent is the efficiency of the Israeli army and border patrol.

The extent to which imprisonment serves as a supplementary deterrent is uncertain, particularly for those offenders who are inspired by Arab nationalist sentiments. No systematic efforts are made by prison officials to re-orient them. They cannot be treated as prisoners of war. But what can be done has not yet been a subject of systematic inquiry. There is no prison treatment program aimed to deal with this type of adventurer or "idealist" who knows himself to be violating laws which he does not regard as morally binding. His deviancy is less often personal and more often a reflection of unsettled political conditions.

Short-Term Imprisonment

Imprisonment is imposed on only a minority of the offenders and, usually, for a short period of time. Of 3,171 persons imprisoned for criminal acts in 1958, the vast majority (88 per cent) were sentenced for less than a year.[18] Most of them (2,169) spent less than three months in prison. Israeli prisons serve both as jails and as penitentiaries. Prisons also are used to coerce recalcitrant persons to pay fines, debts or alimony obligations. In 1958, there were 717 Jews serving time for such civil law violations. All but eight of these convictions were for fewer than three months. None of the prisoners was an Arab — and Arabs compose about 10 per cent of Israel's population.

17. David Ben-Gurion, "Achievements and Tasks of our Generation," *Israel Government Yearbook,* 5722 (1961-62). Jerusalem: Government Printer, 1962, xxxvii.
18. *Ibid.,* Table 49.

TABLE 2[19]

Use of Imprisonment and Other Penalties by Israeli Courts, 1958

Sentence	Number of Convictions
Imprisonment Only	2,245
Imprisonment plus Fine	305
Choice of Prison or Fine	10,870
Chose Prison	585
Chose Fine	8,390
Choice not Known	1,895
Fine Only	22,565
Other Penalties	4,925
Total Convictions	40,910

How can such a short sentence policy be maintained? In 1958, there were twelve convictions for murder, three for attempted murder, seven for manslaughter and seventy-nine for causing death by carelessness, including motor vehicle accidents. There were 329 sentences for offenses against morality, but only nine involved rape or attempted rape. In addition, 3,176 persons were convicted of doing serious harm or assault, 326 of other crimes against persons. Twenty-six persons were convicted of corruption in office; 112 of perjury. Offenses against property were the most common, 24,267 cases. The remaining imprisoned offenders violated state security regulations. Among them are "tough" felons who represent a clear and present danger to society. But prison officials are agreed that they account for fewer than 100 of all inmates.

The imposition of short sentences, even for a few of the security regulation violators, is often explained by welfare considerations. While a man is in prison his whole family suffers. Public welfare payments are a most inadequate economic substitute for the offender's earning power. In the words of one supervising justice: "Whenever possible, the judges seem to accept explanations to be lenient. The Supreme Court has often criticized them for this, but when cases come before them, they too are lenient."

The judges of Israel tend to be partisans of a humanitarian philosophy. Most of them are long-time residents of Israel who are deeply identified with the ideals of Jewish national rebirth. Reformation and rehabilitation are the essence of this movement. Judges are appointed

19. *Criminal Statistics in Israel,* Tables 33 and 82. The imposition of imprisonment or fine may be accompanied by some other measure, such as recognizance or conditional imprisonment.

24

TABLE 3

Israeli Prison Convictions in Relation to
Total Offenses Recorded, 1958[20]

Type of Offense	Total Known Offenses	Number Without a Discovered Suspect	Number Convicted to Serve in Prison
Against the Person (Subtotal)	8,866	1,746	431[21]
Murder[22]	30	12	19
Attempted Murder	61	19	4
Manslaughter	9	3	10
Causing Death by Carelessness	26	1	16
Bodily Harm and Assault	8,740	1,711	382
Against Morality (Subtotal)	1,259	181	146
Against Property (Subtotal)	24,758	18,142	733
Robbery and Attempted Robbery	67	27	2
Thefts	18,570	13,798	399
Receiving and Possession of Stolen Property	402	17	26
Housebreaking and Preparation therefore	5,643	4,260	172
Arson and Causing Damage to Property	76	40	?
Frauds and Forgery	917	181	64
Other Offenses[23]	12,520	821	2,221
Total — All Offenses	48,320	21,071	3,812

20. *Criminal Statistics in Israel,* Tables 10 and 93.

21. Persons sent to prison for detention or because of conviction in 1958 are only approximately comparable to those who were known to have committed a crime in 1958. Some persons accused or convicted of a crime before 1958 went to prison during that year. Others who were accused or convicted in 1958 did not go to prison until 1959 or later.

22. There is a discrepancy of one in the total number of murders in Tables 10 and 93.

23. Variations in classifications required the combining of all other offenses. This category includes economic offenses, emergency regulation violations, unlawful possessions of firearms and all others.

by the President upon nomination by a judges nomination board, after a careful screening process for technical competency.[24] While political factors play a part in the appointment process, they rarely are a consideration except in the choice between alternate, well-qualified persons.

Judges are likely to rely heavily in their sentencing on social-economic and psychological information furnished by probation officers who are employees of the Ministry of Welfare. The probation officers are supervised by social workers, and they are jurisdictionally independent of the courts. They can express their professional judgment independently, as professional specialists. In the Juvenile Court, no child can be adjudged without a prior probation report. No adult criminal under twenty-one can be sentenced to more than a year in prison without such report. Judges are free to ignore all or part of a probation officer's report, but they tend to make much use of it. In 1958, when the courts convicted 40,910 persons, the adult probation department made 880 investigations and supervised 781 convicted, but non-imprisoned offenders.[25]

Mandatory minimum sentences are established for only a few types of cases. Anyone who tries to bribe a public official must be given a prison sentence, as must persons who assault a policeman or are convicted a second time of using explosives to catch fish. Judges cannot change such minimum sentences, but they can suspend them. Under a suspended sentence, a culprit need not go to prison unless he violates the law during the period of his suspended sentence.

Imprisonment as Treatment

Only a minority of offenders require close surveillance to protect them and society from physical harm. They, as well as the remainder, who are less dangerous, are taken out of circulation when they are imprisoned. Most of them will experience this as a severe punishment. It deprives them of freedoms to which all other citizens are entitled. But has there been actualization of the hope held out by Herzl and other humanists all over the world that prisons might make "men again out of the scum of mankind"?

The answer to this question can not be known until pertinent follow-

24. The judges nomination board is presided over by the Minister of Justice, one other Cabinet Minister elected by the Cabinet, the President of the Supreme Court, two other justices elected by that court, two members of the legislature (*Knesseth*) and two practicing members of the bar appointed by the bar council. This nomination procedure is based on the theory that all branches of government, the judiciary, the legislature and the executive, as well as the practicing bar, have a voice in influencing the appointment of judges. The Minister of Justice and the President of the Supreme Court have each a concurrent right to propose candidates to the judges nomination board. The President has no discretion in the matter but must carry out the recommendations of the board.

25. Schmelz and D. Salzman, *op. cit.,* Table 105.

up evidence is collected. But systematic efforts are made to utilize imprisonment for resocialization efforts. The present survey could not analyze them in detail, nor assess their impact on inmates. Instead, it concentrates on the identification of organizational indices of the importance attached to treatment objectives. They include the following:

1.   Treatment specialists are well represented in top level management parts of the system. The scientific director is a reform rabbi, turned criminologist, educator and social worker. He is dedicated to the objective of converting prisons into treatment institutions. The chief social worker, trained in the United States, is imbued with the same objective. The chief psychiatrist regards his prison assignment as a therapeutic mission. Two of the three members of the Release Board are treatment specialists.

2.   A psycho-social classification unit studies all prisoners committed for more than three months.

3.   A separate unit, headed by Chief Psychiatrist David Rosner, treats severely disturbed and aggressive inmates.

4.   Among the 635 prison officials are twenty-one social workers, many of them women, six education officers, four full-time physicians and twenty-four male nurses, plus workshop supervisors. In addition the Ministry of Health pays the salaries of two psychiatrists, one psychiatric social worker and six male psychiatric nurses to assist the prison service in keeping serious psychopathic cases in their custody.

Only a minority of inmates remain in prison long enough for officials to plan comprehensive treatment of the problems they bring with them. Through academic and vocational education, many leave prison with more skills than when they entered. Social workers and psychiatrists are available to help them in facing psycho-social problems. Whether these treatment resources are sufficient to accomplish this objective is among the controversial questions that are openly discussed. No one in a position of administrative responsibility expressed doubt that they are a desirable part of the prison service. But many question how far the treatment point of view should be allowed to mitigate the punitive and retributive aspects of imprisonment. Supreme Court Justice Haim Cohn addressed this question in detail in an opinion denying the appeal of a woman sentenced to life imprisonment for poisoning her lover's wife.

The defense of irresistible impulses has now become part and parcel of the criminal law of Israel . . . but it needs careful definition, in order that the reform which had been intended for relief in justice of diseased persons, should not operate to set the whole criminal law at nought.
Our premise is that every criminal (I mean those grave offenders who are popularly referred to as criminals) acts on impulses, also known as the "evil urges": the very character of these impulses, and the nature of their acts, bear testimony to

27

a deviation from the normal. There is not only the deviation from the conventions of society which found their expression in legal norms, but also a deviation from the normal and average standards of mental health. The old saying, that nobody sins unless the devil rides him, means nothing more than that sinning is always *prima facie* evidence of anormal impulses . . . .

With the progress of medical science, we are now blessed with a psychiatric terminology which is apt to mislead: simple and self-evident things like those I mentioned, may be expressed in technical language and thereby falsely alarm the layman (judges included). You are led to believe that what the experts say in their own terms, is the diagnosis of a disease — only because you don't know, what they know, that actually there is nobody in this modern world of ours who has not at some time or another shown "aggressive impulses," "neurotic tendencies," "compulsion ideas," "hallucinatory dreams or visions," or "ambivalent feelings," and by whatever other names the sufferings of neurotics and temporarily disturbed persons may be called. As far as criminals are concerned, any such symptoms in them are mostly irrelevant for the determination of their responsibility, by whatever name you may choose to call the impulses born of any such anormal causes; or else there would not remain any criminal with responsibility for his acts . . . .

The appellant before us may well, in the eyes of the doctors, be a "sick" person, if any deviation from the normal is indeed to be regarded as sickness; but in the eyes of the law she is not inflicted with any "mental disease." No doubt she is a neurotic; her heart is sick from love ("pathological dependence on her lover") and from disappointment ("depressions, destructive tendencies," etc.), and she was not capable to master her evil impulses: that is the sad lot of all those who stray from the right path and give way to their criminal impulses; and it is for them that the criminal law was made, so that they be punished and deterred.[26]

In Israel, as in all countries, the issue between criminal responsibility and the psychiatric explanation that men act under impulses beyond their control remains unsolved. The dilemma was well summarized by Chief Justice Earl Warren, who, as governor of California, presided over that state's extensive reform of the correctional system: "The idea of punishment has not and cannot be entirely abandoned. It should, however, be regarded as one of the many possible devices for discipline, treatment and ultimately rehabilitation." [27]

Alternatives to Imprisonment

Crime control in Israel relies primarily on fines, probation,[28] suspended sentences, daytime imprisonment and warning or recognizance.[29] The method saves taxpayers a good deal of money because the average cost of keeping a prisoner is 330 Israeli pounds a month ($110), a sum greater than the monthly net income (after deductions) of the majority of prison officers. Fines are often imposed in criminal cases because

26. State of Israel, Official Law Reports, Vol. 16 (1962), 1111.

27. Norman Fenton, *Group Counseling, a Preface to Its Use in Correctional and Welfare Agencies,* Sacramento, California: The County Project in Correctional Methods of the Institute for the Study of Crime and Delinquency, 1961.

28. *Criminal Statistics in Israel, op. cit.,* Tables 33, 82, 106, 218. Included in these statistics were 136 investigations begun in 1958 but not completed. Of the persons supervised, on probation were 523 cases carried at the end of the year, plus 258 who were terminated during 1958.

29. An obligation of record that the convicted person meet specified conditions, such as keeping the peace or paying a certain debt.

judges think they will have a strong deterrent effect. They punish both the culprit and his family by reducing their economic status, but offenders do not lose their livelihood. They can continue to care for their families without becoming public charges.

Fines are the rule in most white-collar crimes, such as income tax violation and fraud. Traffic offenses are punished by fines and, in case of severe or frequent lesser violations, by the cancellation of licenses. A report in 1962 stated:

During the past year 2,000 driving licenses were cancelled or withdrawn, some through administrative channels and some by order of the law. These figures were unfortunately not made public. A special problem are the public transport drivers, the greatest culprits being the owners of taxis who commit crimes against their passengers such as, e.g., stealing from a passenger's luggage or attempting rape. Should such a driver be permitted to work after the completion of the sentence? In many cases the judge did not cancel the license or cancelled it for a short period only. Till recently there was no set procedure for a case of this type. The licensing department requested permission to cancel this type of license with the privilege of retaining the right of appeal to the court. There is now a joint discussion with police headquarters regarding this problem.[30]

The use of fines for offenses which can also be dealt with by imprisonment provides the basis for comparative study of these alternate modes of deviancy control. No such research is now going on, but Israeli judges seem to have much confidence in the deterrent effect of fines and other alternatives to incarceration. Fines are imposed in over 75 per cent of all convictions for serious offenses.

Suspended Sentencing

Provisions for suspended sentences were incorporated in Israel's penal law in 1954. An explanatory preamble to the law before its enactment claimed that this method "has all the advantages of the deterrent effect of a severe sentence of imprisonment without the disadvantages of incarcerating first offenders into prisons. The offender's knowledge that the suspended penalty will be carried out if he offends again will deter him from committing further offenses." [31] After the first year, the Attorney General of Israel, who had supported this reform, reported: "The courts have imposed hundreds of suspended sentences; but only in two cases had the sentence to be carried out owing to subsequent conviction." [32]

Suspended sentences can be imposed for all offenses except pre-

30. The Institute of Criminology at the Hebrew University and the National Council for the Prevention of Accidents, *Proceedings of the Seminar on Road Accidents in Israel,* Jerusalem: Institute for Criminology, 1962, Publication No. 2, XV.
31. Shlomoh Shoham and Moshe Zandberg, "Suspended Sentences in Israel: An Evaluation of the Preventive Efficacy of Prospective Imprisonment," Ramat Gan, Israel: Bar-Ilan University, 1960 (mimeographed).
32. Haim H. Cohn, *op. cit.,* 6.

meditated murder, where a life sentence is mandatory. Suspensions are widely used. There were an average of 3,510 cases a year during the two-year period of 1955-56, and their number has increased since then. Not only first offenders, but recidivists are given this privilege. Older suspended offenders and those who had never been convicted of any crime were, however, far less likely to run afoul of the law again than those with one or more prior offenses.[33]

In selected cases, the district superintendent of police has the authority to allow a resident from his area who has been sentenced for fewer than three months to serve his term by performing clerical, janitorial and other services while living at home. The offenders report to a designated police station for six days a week from 8 A.M. to 2 P.M., the length of the normal work day. In the afternoon and evening he can look after his family and business affairs.

Sentence Remission

Prison terms can be reduced by one-third by action of the Sentence Reviewing Board. Additional reductions are achieved in some cases by appeal of court verdicts or by Presidential pardon. Sentences for somewhat more than 50 per cent of all persons serving for three or more months are reduced on the basis of good behavior in prison and a favorable program for adjustment, or for compassionate reasons.

In spite of vigorous urging by social workers, judges and prison officials for a statewide parole service, there is none. The vacuum is filled in part by a voluntary group, the Society for the Rehabilitation of Prisoners.[34] In Israel, as in nineteenth-century America, a citizen group exercises political influence in the direction of penal reforms. The society, which receives a modest government subsidy, offers limited social services. It is staffed by volunteers and by two social workers, whose salaries are paid by the Prison Service, to offer counsel in the larger cities to a small number of ex-offenders with a "good risk" prognosis. Prison system social workers often help inmates find a job before their release. The army will accept ex-convicts. But as Lester Jaffe and his colleagues point out, "The vast percentage of discharged prisoners in Israel leave prison as alone with their feelings as when they entered; the problems of the past still to be sorted out and waiting ahead, the test of transition

33. *Ibid.,* 14.

34. The society functions like the British John Howard and the American prison societies that emerged during the 18th and 19th centuries. They exercise a major influence on public officials in behalf of penal reform. Members of the society inspect prisons and call attention to conditions which they believe to require change. They also offer limited social services to selected offenders and their dependents.

from prison to free society." [35] Many fail to pass this test. How many no one knows, but nearly 45 per cent of all serious offenders were recidivists, although not necessarily guilty of the same offense.

Interestingly enough, recidivists are overrepresented among persons sentenced to serve in prison. This finding suggests that Israeli judges may be differentiating fairly well between offenders who can be dealt with outside prisons and those who cannot. Yet there is no significant difference between the proportion of recidivists in the offense categories for which data are available.[36] Would there be more or fewer recidivists if Israeli penal practices were different? Law enforcement officials can do no more than speculate about the answer to this crucial question. Data to answer it are not available — not in Israel, nor anywhere else in the world.

In general, the courts find it possible to deal with the great majority of criminals through other than long-term removal from society. At any one time, on a cumulative basis the inmate population includes a larger proportion of long-termers than those convicted to such terms in any one year. But of the 1,124 persons in Israeli prisons at the end of 1958, 440 or 39 per cent, had court sentences of less than a year. Only 27 per cent, 144 Jewish and 154 non-Jewish (mostly Arab) prisoners had been sentenced for over three years. Less than 8 per cent, a total of 99 Israelis, were serving terms of over ten years.

Prison Furloughs

Imprisonment in Israel does not necessarily imply complete cessation of direct contact with the world outside. There is a liberal visiting and letter-writing policy. In 1958, the Minister of Police was also given authority to grant brief furloughs from imprisonment.

The furlough program aims to reduce the prospects that long-term imprisonment will impair family and community ties on which convicts depend when they are ultimately released. For family festivities or funerals, Arab or Jewish religious holidays, inmates can request a furlough up to four times a year. If recommended by the director of their prison, approval of these requests by the Minister of Police has been

35. Lester D. Jaffe, Zvi Givati, Chava Lehman and Yitzchak Bakal, "Legitimizing After-Care for Institutionalized Adult Offenders in Israel," Jerusalem, Israel: The Hebrew University, 1961 (mimeographed), 1.

36. Recidivism of Serious Offenders in Israel, 1958
(In per cent)

	First Offenders	Recidivists
Total Offenses (N = 14,094)	55	45
Of these		
Against Persons (N = 3,513)	58	42
Against Morality (N = 324)	48	52

From Criminal Statistics in Israel, 1949-1958, op. cit., Table 49. Recidivists were not defined. They are not necessarily persons previously committed for the same offense.

31

given in all cases. If it is refused, the prisoner is entitled to an explanation. About 600 such furloughs have been granted in recent years for as long a period as ninety-six hours. Only five prisoners failed to return. Four of them were rearrested and one is not accounted for.[37]

There is much favorable speculation about the impact of this furlough policy on prisoner adjustment both in prison and after release. It seems plausible to assume that periodic leaves make it easier to maintain family ties. Convicts can also look for a job before they get out. This is all the more important since Israel does not have a nationwide adult parole service. Furlough prospects are believed to provide a strong positive incentive for inmates to accept prison rules and discipline and to have a strong morale effect on inmates with good family relationships, whose absences are experienced as hardships by their wives, children and others. Furloughs also may help to reduce the pressure on inmates and their spouses outside to engage in deviant sexual behavior.

Prison and social welfare officials are cognizant of the experimental value of the country's prison furlough policy, but hard evidence to assess its impact on inmates and their adjustment is lacking. Research funds are no more available for this purpose than for the investigation of many other fundamental questions of penal policy.

A Question of Effectiveness

What is the effectiveness of Israel's policy of predominantly non-institutional management of criminals? Are law and order breaking down when the bulk of criminals are fined or sentenced to conditional imprisonment, or when those sentenced to prison can look forward to being released within a short time? Israeli criminal statistics are not being collected to provide pertinent data. There have been no follow-up studies of convicted criminals to relate their sentences to subsequent adjustment. Nothing is known about what type of criminal may be more likely to reform with the aid of a compassionate approach and what type might abuse so compassionate a penal system.

It is unlikely that the system is equally suitable for all types of offenders. Israeli prisoners can be grouped into three broad categories from the point of how their rehabilitation potential is affected by the country's penal policy:

1. *Sinners*: Offenders who share society's condemnation of their act. They share the predominant values of the social system and there-

37. Since 1944 the governor of Mississippi has granted "Christmas leaves" for up to ten days. Superintendent C. E. Breazeale of the Mississippi State Penitentiary reports in a personal communication that "90% return on time and 95% return without having to be apprehended."

32

fore feel guilty about their deviant acts.

2. *Idealists*: Offenders who evaluate positively the act for which they were condemned by society. They have different values and feel no guilt regarding their conduct.

3. *Sociopaths*: Offenders without a well-defined social value system. They are motivated largely by self-needs. They are not concerned with society's value expectation and have no guilt feelings.

Israel's compassionate and rehabilitative orientation facilitates the early status restoration of sinner-type criminals, those who commit thefts, crimes of passion or embezzlements about which they feel guilty.

Idealistic offenders are taken out of circulation for a period, but other than humane treatment during their incarceration, nothing is planned (and often nothing can be done) to bring about a shift in their value orientation. They are persons who assault and murder to defend their family honor. There are also isolated cases of fanatically religious Jews, who damage the property of Sabbath violators, or a case of kidnapping a child from his non-religious parents in order to make sure that he would receive an Orthodox upbringing. Also included in this category are political offenders, who are in contact on security matters with countries unfriendly to Israel. A few are Jews; the majority are Arabs who spy, cross borders illegally, carry arms and explosives, commit sabotage and even murder for what they regard as patriotic motives. Imprisonment may make such rebels more cautious but by itself is not likely to bring about a change in the ideals that led to their crime. The prevention of recidivism among those persons is primarily a police and security problem.

Sociopathic criminals present a management problem in every penal system. One wonders if under Israel's compassionate policies many will not be released before a comprehensive treatment effort can be made to reach them. While no proved methods exist to make an impact on such persons, a short-term prison policy does not allow enough time for a meaningful confrontation with predominant social values through treatment programs.

While there can be only speculation about the impact of the country's penal system on these different types of offenders, one fact stands out: Israeli prison officials and the general public express only mild concern over the general level of public safety. Penal policy is largely a nonpartisan issue. There is no organized crime in Israel. Criminal gangs are uncommon. The police are vigilant. Prosecutors are active in bringing before a court those suspected of criminal acts. One can travel in Israel by day and by night without fear. Here and there one hears expressions of concern over the increasing frequency of reported juvenile delinquency and adult criminal behavior. While crime rates are relatively low in comparison to many modern countries, in 1958 there were reports of 30 murders, 85 cases of rape, attempted rape, and sodomy with force, including 20 that involved children as victims. Any one of these cases, when reported in the press, gives rise to understandable anxiety about the state of public safety.

The predominant mood of the country, however, is that law and order are assured within what are regarded as normally expected numbers of deviations. In addition to ordinary crimes deeply mourned casualties occur during each year of battle with Arab border patrols and infiltrators from hostile countries. But they have been reduced greatly, especially since the Sinai campaign in 1956, when the Gaza strip was temporarily occupied where Egyptian sabotage units (*Feddahin*) had been stationed. Its borders are now patrolled by United Nations troops, and the Jewish and Druse-Arab patrol units have prevented any major breakthrough of unfriendly troops.

Security and Reform

On August 1, 1958, a mass prison break occurred at Shatta. The break had been organized by incarcerated Egyptian intelligence agents who took advantage of loose security precautions. Sixty-six Arab infiltrators and smugglers escaped across the Jordan border less than three miles away. In pitched battles, which followed the mutiny, two guards and eleven inmates were killed.

Basic penal policy issues were publicly aired for the first time in a subsequent investigation of the circumstances leading to this crisis. In the words of a *Jerusalem Post* editorial:

Prisons are a disagreeable subject and nobody in this country has ever cared to have much to do with them. In the old days when the Jewish Agency operated a shadow government side by side with that of the Mandatory administration there were Jewish schools and Jewish hospitals, but no Jewish prisons. There was no need for them.[1]

While the Shatta incident focused some attention on the diverse problems involved in running a modern prison system, most of the concern was with security precautions. After hearing testimony from forty-eight witnesses, the investigating commission concluded: "It is obvious from the evidence, including that of the Arab prisoners, that it was not hardship at the prison which led to the break . . . . The break was the inescapable result of the indifference to the most elementary security rules." [2]

Ladders were left in the prison yard, and dangerous building materials such as steel rods were within easy access of all inmates. A gate key was entrusted to a convicted infiltrator and spy. The key to the arms storeroom was kept where prisoners could see it. Senior officers of the prison were in the habit of leaving the prison every Thursday afternoon, and all inmates knew this. Some of the guards had never learned how to handle guns.

Security, Humanism and Professionalism

The Shatta incident refocused the relative priority of security considerations. It was seen by the public primarily as a blow to the organizational prestige of the Prison Service. A number of officers and guards at Shatta and the deputy director responsible for security had to resign.

Security considerations have remained high in the hierarchy of policy objectives. In 1962, all but one of Israel's six prison installations

1. Accounts of the Shatta crisis and its investigation by a committee headed by Judge Dr. Moshe Etzioni are based on accounts in the *Jerusalem Post,* between August 4, and September 22, 1958. The two other members were highly regarded members of parliament, Y. Klebanoff and Y. Ben Aharon.
2. *Ibid.*

were administered under medium- and close-security precautions,[3] although only a handful—certainly fewer than 100 inmates—were believed to constitute a potential danger to public order or to national security. Nine out of ten of the prisoners served sentences of less than a year, and furloughs were granted periodically to many of those who had sentences of over six months. Nevertheless, extensive and expensive security precautions were taken while the prisoners were under sentence.

The average inmate population remained stable between 1958 and 1962 — around 1100 and 1200. But the number of prison system employees rose by one-third, from 475 to 635. The additional 160 officers were nearly all guards and officials concerned with security matters. Only six education officers were added to enhance the system's manpower concerned with treatment programs.

Between 1952 and 1958, the prison commissioner placed high priority on the introduction of professional standards for the psychosocial treatment of inmates. Security precautions were largely delegated to the deputy commissioner, an experienced army officer who had been a major in the military police.

The Shatta incident had other consequences. It brought public attention to the system's humanistic orientation. The hero of the Shatta riot was a Jewish murderer, who had been sentenced to die in 1953 for shooting his father; when Israel abolished the death penalty for murder, his sentence was commuted to life imprisonment. At great personal risk, this "lifer" attacked the Egyptian ringleader and, together with another prisoner and one guard, locked him in his cell. Later, when the prison guards lost control of the situation, the convicted murderer jumped over a prison wall, hailed a passing taxi and asked to be driven to the nearest police station. He returned with several officers and helped them to subdue escaped inmates. An Israeli Arab, also sentenced to life imprisonment for murder, defended two of the Jewish wardens with a pair of scissors, thus saving their lives.

The Shatta investigation did not lead to suggestions that prisons be made "tougher" for the inmates. It did not retard judicial reliance on alternatives to imprisonment as means to control criminal deviants. The

3. The terms *minimum, medium* and *close* security are used here in their technical meaning, as defined in the *Manual of Correctional Standards,* issued by the American Correctional Association, New York: 1960, 211. *Minimum custody:* Inmates are considered eligible for outside of prison assignment, such as farms, camps, logging operations, etc., and are usually under general or intermittent supervision only. *Medium custody:* Inmates are available for work on the inside of prison without constant and direct supervision and on the outside of the regular enclosure under supervision. *Close custody:* Inmates are housed in the institution's most secure housing units, are employed in the institution's enclosure and are under constant supervision.

Prison Service was able to get higher budgetary allocations which in part were invested in plant improvements that contribute to inmate comfort and welfare. The investigation did, however, make prison administrators very sensitive about any treatment proposal that would require a lowering of security precautions.

The emphasis on protecting the organizational status of the Prison Service for its capability to control inmates did not do away with the expectation that it also maintain a treatment and resocialization program. The director of the women's prison had to resign when a newspaper story disclosed that she was too hard as a disciplinarian. While the prison commissioner, Dr. Zvi Hermon, was criticized for "concentrating his attention on rehabilitation and social work, at the expense of security matters," which were left largely to his deputy, no one questioned the importance of the professional mission to which he had dedicated himself. Dr. Hermon was relieved of responsibility for security and personnel policies but was appointed to a new post, that of scientific director.

In this role, he retains responsibility for the development of the very function in which he has a primary interest: the classification of inmates, the expansion of work and treatment programs and the planning of rehabilitation services. He has administrative supervision of all professional services, medical, social service, vocational training, education and research. He also continues to represent the prison commissioner on the board to review requests for release by deserving prisoners who have served two-thirds of their sentences. In organizational terms, this change was a demotion from a first to a second echelon job. In functional terms, it freed the former commissioner from many administrative responsibilities. It left him more time to concentrate on the attainment of higher professional standards in the Prison Service. But it reduced his authority to allocate scarce budgetary resources for the attainment of these professional goals.

The Ascendancy of Security

Managerial responsibility, highly concentrated before Shatta, is now more diversified. Security objectives are in ascendancy. Aryeh Nir, a high police official, was appointed to the post of commissioner. A new deputy, also with a police background, was appointed to handle security matters, personnel policies, finance and supply problems. In theory, there is broad agreement among these policy makers that prisons should be more than institutions for the humane warehousing of inmates. But they differ in their priorities.

Illustrative of this policy is the fate of an experimental outside work program. A group of youthful offenders at Tel Mond had been allowed to hold regular jobs outside of the prison, returning there at night on their own. Those responsible for this venture were strongly convinced of the program's rehabilitative impact. It required the youths to do meaningful work in the community under normal working conditions; it forced them to exercise self-control and self-discipline. The penal officials believed that this program was a better preparation for life than incarceration behind a barbed wire stockade. There were no serious violations of trust by the youths. Nevertheless, discontinuation of the program was ordered after the "Shatta Incident." The new prison commissioner believed that the risk should not be taken; he feared that some of the youths would run away or commit another crime while working on the outside.

There also has been a slowing-down in the expansion of treatment programs since 1958. Social service personnel have not been increased. Before the Shatta incident, plans had been made to introduce group counselling. Dr. Norman Fenton, then associate director for classification and treatment of the California department of correction, the chief advocate of this treatment, had been invited to come to Israel as a consultant. His guidebook[4] had been translated into Hebrew by Mrs. Victoria Nissim, the chief social worker of the prison system, who completed graduate training in the United States. Final arrangements for this consultation were not completed after the Shatta incident.

The security and treatment officials differ not in absolutes, but in their priorities. The present commissioner is identified with a humanitarian orientation and is theoretically in favor of turning prisons into institutions for psycho-social treatment. Security and treatment considerations compete in the market place of thought in all of the prison system's top policy officials who were interviewed by the writer.

Crisis-Impact on the Evaluation of Organizational Effectiveness
The goals of imprisonment include safety, treatment and organizational objectives. There is no single standard for evaluating the effectiveness of a prison; many accomplishments are aimed for. Some are primarily related to the public image that prisons protect society and that they be run with predictability. Others deal more with productivity norms — what is done to change the inmates. Most officials subscribe to all of these objectives, but differ in the relative importance that they attach to their attainment:

4. Norman Fenton, *An Introduction to Group Counseling in Prison,* Sacramento, California: Department of Correction, 1955. Group counselling normally uses correctional officers as discussion leaders of groups of inmates. They talk about their personal problems and adjustment prospects after leaving prisons.

Safety Objectives:
1. Protection from dangerous convicted criminals.
2. Safekeeping of persons who are imprisoned from themselves and revenge by others.
3. Safety of prison staff from attack by inmates.

Organizational Objectives:
4. Success in gaining added resources to improve prison facilities.
5. Optimum use of budget.
6. Organizational capability to attract and keep personnel who are adequately trained for their complex assignments.
7. Staff work without disabling jurisdictional disputes within the organization.
8. Organizational awareness of the existence of unresolved problems, along with planned efforts to surmount them.

Treatment Objectives:
9. Re-education of inmates to reduce the probability of their becoming recidivists.
10. Teaching of work and educational skills to add to the capabilities of inmates to earn a good income.
11. Humane policies.
12. Influence on inmates to identify themselves with the expectation of lawful conduct, held by prison officials and the general public.
13. Possibility of releasing most inmates before the expiration of their sentences without unreasonable risks to public safety.

The Shatta incident led only to partial examination of how other organizational objectives had been met. Among the consequences of this orientation were a heightened concern with safety objectives and relatively less emphasis on what was being accomplished to meet treatment objectives. The system, evaluation showed, had not been able to attract enough of the skilled and professionally motivated manpower to form prisons into secure *and* therapeutic milieus. Funds to hire key security personnel had been withheld. Some guards were untrained for even the more rudimentary parts of their job. There was much evidence that prison officials were aware of these problems. They were mentioned, but there was no thorough survey of organizational effectiveness.

No such study is being planned. Prison administrators, like those of most large organizations, are pressed somewhat beyond their resources to meet day-to-day operational objectives. In the absence of any new public crisis since Shatta, the image of the prison system as a safe organization has been restored. There has been no public clamor to examine penal policies in terms of productivity objectives. Only in the exceptional organization — in Israel as everywhere — is research to evaluate programs part of the basic administrative structure.[5]

Reference Group Differences

There are indications of the existence of fairly consistent differences in preferences among policy-making officials in the prison system's central headquarters staff, prison directors, Israeli judges, and policy-making officials in the Ministry of Justice and Social Welfare. While no systematic survey of attitudes was made, interviews with two dozen officials suggest that it is analytically useful to differentiate between *military pioneers* and *human relations specialists*.

The *military pioneers* identify with Israel's principal power group, who are socialist-idealists. They have always wanted to settle the land and to expand its capabilities through the absorption of immigrants and their own labor. While many of them came from middle class homes, with an emphasis on education, they placed primary stress on having technical and manual skills in farming, carpentry and other trades. The pressure of political events forced some of them to divert an increasing amount of their energy to military and underground activities during the decade before the establishment of the state. The very survival of the Jewish homeland was dependent upon them.

Few of these military pioneers completed their university educations. But they were the core of the country's pioneer elite — the *Chalutzim*. They volunteered to serve in the British armed forces in World War II; at the same time, they were part of the Jewish self-defense force. Often they engaged in dangerous and clandestine activities, transporting immigrants to Palestine or smuggling arms into villages that would otherwise have been at the mercy of Arab guerila forces.

The military pioneers are not unsympathetic to social welfare objectives. They believe that the attainment of such ends should be conditioned first and foremost by safety considerations. They place great value on discipline, careful planning and a high degree of predictability in the organization of administrative responsibilities.

The prisons' welfare services are staffed primarily by *human relations specialists,* whose reference group is scientific and professional rather than military. Some of these officials have the same socialist and *Chalutz* orientation as do the majority of military pioneers, but they tend to have more professional education. Many of them practiced their pro-

5. Prison statistics deal primarily with data on intake. What happens to inmates during their incarceration or after their release is less often the object of research. A noteworthy exception to this generalization is the department of correction of California. A special research department was set up in the department to engage in such studies.

fessions before coming to Palestine. They have kept up with professional thinking in psychology, sociology, social work, psychiatry and education. While many have been in a military service and in the underground army, their first and foremost concern in efforts to control deviants is the application of scientific knowledge and professional traditions. They are readers of and contributors to technical journals; they are eager to learn about new research developments, and they see the prison system primarily as a rehabilitative agency. While they accept a dependable state of security as a prerequisite for organizing any prison treatment program, they prefer to rely on psycho-social intervention to attain resocialization goals. They believe that unreasonable security risks are not implied if policies are adopted that turn prisons into reformatories. And they lean on the side of modest risk taking if this is necessary to keep inmates under conditions where their own consciences, rather than the prison guards, must take primary responsibility for the acceptance of prison discipline.

Although these policy divergencies are similar to those found in other countries with a penal reform orientation, in Israel there are few partisans of a punitive approach to penology. Security advocates are not necessarily "tough" on inmates. They stress safety as an organizational prestige necessity, but they do not see it as an alternative goal to treatment. However, in the allocation of scarce budgetary resources and in the hiring of personnel, security qualifications receive much consideration, and there is less money for the expansion of treatment programs.

Symbolic Significance of Security

The security emphasis in a country where most prisoners are kept for less than a year appears to be inconsistent. Why is it deemed necessary to keep inmates under heavy guard when some are allowed to go home on furloughs, when many are released before the end of their sentences, and when few are regarded as dangerous to public safety? Why cannot most inmates be placed in the open-prison farm type institution that Theodor Herzl envisioned in his novel *Alt-Neuland?*

This inconsistency must be viewed within the framework of Israel's recent history. Security in Israel is more than a military necessity. It is a major psychological prop. Virtually from the beginning of the British mandatory regime in 1920, the Jewish population experienced periodic guerilla warfare. Independence was followed by an invasion of troops from seven nearby Arab countries. Any breakdown in security provides reason for concern that others will follow. If prisoners can break out by force from supposedly closely guarded quarters, does this not impugn the capability of the police who are closely identified with the prison administration?

Rational responses do not necessarily answer such questions. Actually, Israel today maintains a state of internal and external security that compares favorably with that of many countries. No amount of security can prevent occasional prison riots and escapes. Repeated incidents of this nature occur in American prisons, including Alcatraz and San Quentin which have security precautions far more rigid than those in any of Israel's prisons.

The security emphasis in Israel's prisons bears an intimate relationship to the general significance of safety in a country that has never known declared peace since its establishment. There are a few ordinary criminals who need careful control. There are security cases — infiltrators, maurauders and saboteurs — who might take advantage of an open prison to escape and to commit new depredations. But for most inmates, no heavy guard or barbed wire barriers are needed to ensure discipline. It is the organization that wishes to be secure from criticism. Such criticism is almost certain if any criminal escapes. If policies are tightened to reduce escape chances — even at the expense of treatment objectives — there is less likelihood of criticism.

Accommodation Versus Innovation

Humanitarianism and security do not prevent crime. Israeli policy makers are aware of this fact. There has been no comprehensive effort to deal with many of the questions that plague prison officials all over the world. Israeli leaders freely admit to a variety of practices which they regard as shortcomings, such as the following:

1. There are no indeterminate sentences to fit the length of the imprisonment to the psycho-social characteristics of the offender and his program of reformation.

2. Existing prisons are old-fashioned and expensive to maintain.

3. There are insufficient minimum custody facilities to house the large majority of inmates, who are imprisoned for short terms of less than a year.

4. There is a shortage of appropriately trained prison personnel.

5. Highly individualized diagnostic reports on every long term offender made at the Observation and Classification Center at Tel Mond are not utilized to any great extent. The prison system cannot now afford to maintain a sufficient variety of specialized treatment programs.

6. There is no statewide adult parole service.[6]

6. A sub-committee of the National Council on Crime and Delinquency is currently assembling information in order to prepare a proposal for the establishment of a parole service.

7. There is no systematic research on the impact of different forms of punishment (including different types of incarceration) on a variety of categories of offenders.[7]

Next to pride of accomplishment, self-criticism is the Israeli's favorite national sport. Prison officials look at their policies as being in transition. Their explanations commute between "look how far we have come" to "we have a long way to go."

The existence of many other problems is acknowledged. For instance, men can be imprisoned for nonpayment of alimony. When this is done, they are usually made indigent, less likely that they can pay alimony. There is ambivalence regarding long term imprisonment of Arab youths who did not engage in espionage or sabotage, but crossed the borders of Israel without permission.

The awareness of policy makers of major discrepancies between these questions and the availability of good answers results in several response patterns. The military pioneer element tends to be predisposed to be *accommodative*. They accept the *status quo,* with periodic efforts to introduce reforms under circumstances not likely to arouse controversy or administrative complications. The more professionally oriented people prefer to be more actively *innovative*. They look for opportunities to experiment. They make proposals, even under controversial circumstances. They take calculated risks of being regarded as "fanatic," "troublesome," and "visionary."

While there are these differences in emphasis between policy makers, there are also many common objectives. Tradition as such does not rank high in either value system. In theory, any practice is subject to change if a rationale can be supplied. High prestige is attached to reforms that can be characterized as "humanitarian" and "progressive." Noteworthy illustrations of this approach are the country's limited use of imprisonment, its short-term policy of incarceration, the prison furlough program, the employment of women social workers in men's prisons, and the acceptance in the army for military service of many ex-convicts.

Risk-taking is a function of prison administrators in Israel as it is everywhere else in the world. Decisions must be made about how to deal

---

7. Existing statistics are primarily descriptive. They focus on non-manipulatable rather than manipulatable variables. *Non-Manipulatable factors*: Circumstances inherent in the phenomenon that do not lend themselves to being changed. Crime rates vary dramatically by age, sex and ethnic affiliation. There are few delinquent pre-teenagers. But one cannot keep children from growing up, turn boys into girls or bring up Jewish slum children like Arab village youngsters who have low crime rates. *Manipulatable factors*: Conditions that can be changed by social and individual action such as the marital stability of parents of law violators. It might be affected by social casework, by adequate housing and by good medical care. The same applies to income. If increased, the pressure of antisocial acts may be lessened by the capability of persons to provide more for their own needs and that of their families.

with criminals, some of whom are feared, many of whom are despised, and others who are pitied. Decisions often must be made on the basis of incomplete evidence, with only clinical experience of uncertain relevancy to guide the policy makers. No one can give absolute assurance that the extension of privileges to convicts might not lead to abuses. While it is more expensive to house inmates in medium- and close-custody institutions, no one can be sure that the transfer of many to minimum-custody settings might not result in mass escapes. Predictions about the future behavior of any particular inmate involve elements of uncertainty.

In theory, none of the policy makers interviewed disagreed with the point of view that it is better to give inmates a chance to demonstrate their capacity to live up to social expectations while still under legal surveillance than to wait until the completion of their sentence and their unconditional release. Chance-taking is one of the chief functions of management. The prison furlough system is an illustration that Israeli prison administrators are willing to take such chances. But the mass escape from Shatta Prison raised questions about the wisdom of this policy. As a result, even the men who go on furlough and return to prison on their own, are usually kept under medium- and close-custody conditions.

Penal innovations are politically circumscribed. They are not "packaged" with general reforms of economic and social conditions that seem to be related to a reduction in the incidence of most crimes: regular employment, adequate education and peace between the Jewish state and its Arab neighbors. This conservative framework of prison reform has to be viewed within the context of the fact that all prison officials are government employees. Their influence and future careers are dependent on acceptance by the political structure. Gradualism rather than urgency has characterized the Israeli reform movement.

There is in Israel a strong reliance on *newism,* an ideology which encourages change. Tradition or the *status quo* is evaluated negatively except in the area of religion. The attribute of novelty is sometimes presumed to indicate validity. While there is intellectual recognition that a new program is not necessarily an improvement over previous conditions or alternate policies, an innovation provides the basis for hope that a more promising solution will emerge. The belief that the new may be "progressive" makes it possible for innovations to survive a developmental period long enough to be perfected technically and to be tested by scientific methods. Also the innovation confers status on the people associated with it and provides an opportunity for new experience. It gives them a sense of achievement and enhances their morale. New policies are pregnant with the possibility of substantive scientific discovery. And in

44

Israel policy makers are keenly looking for the new.

Penal policy is the concern of a wide group of specialists, only some of whom are working for the prison system. In Israel, as in the United States, penal reform is primarily a movement of professionals, although persons outside the prison system are prominently involved. Part of their reform effort is an emphasis on psycho-social treatment and educational techniques.

Concern about the long-run effectiveness of present penal policies is expressed freely. The recorded incidence of juvenile and adult offenses is increasing. The next generation seems to be less idealistic than the old. There is so much less to struggle for. As the challenge for survival lessens, there may be a loss of morals that will be evidenced by an increase in criminal deviancies, as is so in many other lands. Much serious attention in government circles is given to prevent this increase. Prisons are seen as only *one of many* resources to control criminal deviants.

Conclusions

The development of penal policy in Israel can be studied in terms of its uniqueness and the possible generalizations which can be drawn from it. It is unique because Israel emerged as a modern state built from nothing but a blueprint. The motion was conceived by self-made men from all parts of the world and implemented by volunteers and voluntary contributions. Many seemingly insurmountable economic, health, political and military obstacles had to be overcome. While the British government, the League of Nations and the United Nations provided legal sanction for this development, the actual institution building was done by self-selected pioneers from such diverse places as Pinsk, Plonsk, London, Berlin, Paris, Johannesburg, Baghdad and New York. In these respects, and some others, Israel is unique. And there is much uniqueness about its prisons.

But every human institution also bears some likeness to others that perform the same function. This study of Israel's prisons was in part undertaken to identify possible generalizations that can be deduced from one case and checked for the applicability to other emerging countries.

Low Priority of Prison Services

Government involves the political enforcement of priorities. Prisons have a low priority among the welfare institutions which the state provides to meet the needs of its citizens. While long-range planning, innovation and experimentation were characteristic of many facets of Israel's public life, its prisons developed largely on the basis of improvisation. This value judgment had three consequences for penal policy:

1. The new prison system was built on the organizational pattern established by the mandatory government, although the state of Israel emerged on the basis of objection to the way this government had used its authority. For instance, penal affairs were left under the jurisdiction of three cabinet members. Most of the laws governing prisons were left intact. New social institutions do not develop after a revolution or independence, unless such change was a focus of the struggle.

2. There was no prior legislative study of prison policy. Developments were heavily dependent on the initiative and concerns of those who were given administrative responsibility.

3. No cadre of experts was trained before the establishment of the state to be ready to organize the prison system.

46

Functional Changes within a Traditional Structure

While the legal structure is traditional, with modifications that increase each year, the system's spirit reflects the ethos of the new state. A predominantly punitive approach was replaced by one that is humanitarian. Well-established penal practices were modified by the application of professional standards, within the framework of a scientific ideology. Rationality rather than revenge is the principal method for weighing alternate prison policies. These changes in emphasis are reflected in the abolition of the death penalty, except for genocide and treason, and the abolition of flogging.

The new state, as the mandatory government did, uses prisons to combat efforts at undermining the government. But there have been major shifts in what is regarded as subversive and treasonable.

Social and rehabilitative services are understaffed. Such programs as the establishment of work camps in the as yet unreclaimed desert, of halfway houses in the cities and of nationwide parole supervision would require major increases in the budget, and there are many other public services which are also starved for funds to make urgently needed innovations. This helps to explain why many penal policy makers are conservative in their advocacy of costly reforms. Most of their energy is expended in keeping the system stable and capable of housing its inmates under conditions least likely to give rise to notoriety.

Technically trained personnel are employed in policy-making positions. This system has resulted in the recruitment of a cadre of highly motivated and well-trained professionals who are attracted by opportunities to apply their professional skills. Such working condition incentives play a big role. Wages of social workers, psychologists and psychiatrists are fairly uniform throughout Israel, because most of them are salaried employees of governmental or quasi-public agencies.

There are modest resources for criminological study, but prison administrators in Israel today face the same fundamental questions that prison reformers are confronted with everywhere. And humane techniques of dealing with inmates are no panacea. Recidivism still characterizes a significant proportion of those who are sent to prison.

Guidelines from Science and Professionalism

The correctional movement in the world has had a clearly defined reform program since 1870. Its precepts have been subscribed to by criminologists of many lands and by delegates to repeated national and international congresses. Yet the implementation of these precepts has been slow. They are opposed by legal traditions, administrative constraints and the absence of well-organized political forces favoring penal reform. The principles of the correctional movement, like all ideologies, are more programmatic than operational. They suggest a sense of direction for changes which are sought to a lesser or greater extent in every part of the world.

Those responsible for penal policy in Israel are knowledgeable about the professional standards advocated by the correctional movement. Such standards have been applied within limits set by financial resources, the availability of trained staff and the general political disinterest in the details of prison management. These trends are reflected by the existence of a decided preference for reformation rather than retribution; the inclination of most Israeli judges to adjust their sentences more to the nature of the criminal than his crime; the employment of a variety of reform-oriented penal policies, including fines, suspended sentences, short-term imprisonment, and sentence remission; the encouragement of communication between the inmates and their families and friends; and the granting of brief furloughs for participation in family festivals and job hunting. (There is, however, only the beginning of parole services. Most prisoners are released without parole supervision.)

The goals of imprisonment include safety, treatment and organizational integrity. There is no single standard for evaluating the effectiveness of a prison. Many accomplishments are aimed for. Some are primarily related to the public image that prisons protect society and that they be run with predictability. Others deal more with productivity norms — what is done to change the inmates. Most officials subscribe to all of these objectives, but vary in the importance which they attach to their attainment. Policy makers are identified with different reference groups orientations, each with somewhat different priorities concerning safety, organizational goals and treatment objectives.

Large scale organizations serve to accomplish these complex tasks through a division of labor. Work is characterized by high predictability, which is necessary if diverse specialists are to work together with efficiency. Stability is a highly prized goal. Drastic changes are most likely to occur after a crisis event which focusses attention on problems that technicians have often identified but could not remedy for lack of attention from policy makers.

Prison officials are aware of the existence of many unresolved problems. But they are pressed beyond their resources to meet day-to-day operational objectives. As a result, there is little systematic study of fundamental penal questions. These are dealt with from time to time on an emergency rather than a planned basis.

Reform or Leniency?

Whenever a crime is committed, the act is of concern to several audiences. How are these audiences or public opinion segments related to Israel's penal policy?

In many a crime there are victims. Their fright, injury and even death cannot be redressed. Damages incurred through robbery and swindle are not undone by the conviction and punishment of the offender. Victims may participate in the penal process as witnesses. They cease to have a role once the accused is declared guilty. Victims have no damages awarded to them. They are forgotten. Instead, attention is focussed on the criminal, who now becomes the "underdog," often to be pitied because of his conviction.

Victims often view such an attitude as unrealistic, if not unjust. It fails to meet the popular expectation that the guilty be punished. They relate the measure of their felt injury to their interpretation of the court's action.

Public opinion leaders, like newspaper editors, judges and law enforcement officers, particularly policemen, have a more general concern for the maintenance of law and order. A trial may, therefore, be viewed as a test of public policy. It dramatizes the degree of vigilance exercised to maintain security.

There is little systematic knowledge about the reaction patterns of victims and the general public. In the long run these are crucial factors. Laws and their enforcement require a supportive public opinion if they are to be effective. This fact is well known in Israel. It is a country in which within the memory of living men resistance to many laws of the previous mandatory and Turkish rulers was seen as patriotism. Law enforcement was systematically undermined.

Ambivalence regarding the enforcement of certain laws is found in every country. But it is not a significant supportive element of penal reform. The leadership of reform movements is in the hands of judges, law enforcement officials and prison officials, who are *not* ambivalent about law enforcement. Penal reformists in Israel as elsewhere are not in favor of leniency as such, but they are in favor of a rational approach to the control of criminal deviants. When leniency is proposed, it is based on evidence or the assumption that lengthy imprisonment or other forms of punishment do not deter others from committing the same crime. Nor do they necessarily facilitate the reform of the criminal. This theory is in conflict with a widely based popular belief that degradation and the denial of privileges have a deterrent effect on many offenders. Whether such deterrence is ever attained is unknown for most categories of of-

49

fenses. But the belief that punishment might deter is important. It rationalizes the existing system of punishment, including imprisonment.

The Minister of Justice expressed criticism of the practice of Israeli courts in consistently handing down sentences far short of the maximum stipulated by the law. He declared that penal policy is the exclusive prerogative of the legislature, not the courts.[1]

The Minister of Justice cited as examples the sentences of a few months' imprisonment given for very serious tax evasion cases, involving hundreds of thousands of pounds, although the maximum penalty for such an offense is four years. His remark addressed itself to an unresolved issue: "Going over hundreds of files, I simply cannot understand a situation where a man who steals one thousand pounds from a neighbor is sent to prison for six months or two years while another who robs the state of vast sums, by tax evasion, gets a few months, even a suspended sentence." [2]

Court sentences are deliberate and highly individual acts by a social system to encourage the maintenance of law and order and a sense of equity in the population. The extent of the achievement of these objectives is a variable that must be taken into account. In the long run, no penal reform can be sustained without a supportive public opinion.

A Laboratory for Research

In September 1962, the Hebrew University played host to the Twelfth International Course in Criminology organized in collaboration with the International Society of Criminology. It addressed itself to problems of causation and prevention of crime in developing countries. Participants from thirty-seven countries adopted a resolution "that the developing countries adopt the system, now operating successfully in Israel, for the training of personnel working in community centers." [3]

1. *The Jerusalem Post Weekly*, Friday, March 22, 1963, 6. News item regarding a seminar on "Penal Reform" held under the auspices of the Hebrew University Institute of Criminology in cooperation with the Ministry of Justice. In the audience were Supreme Court Justices, members of the prosecution, police officers and jurists. The Minister of Justice recognized that unlike the bench the legislature was obviously unable to take into account the circumstances of each case. But he thought the courts were duty-bound to respect the intentions of the law-makers.
2. *Ibid.*
3. International Annals of Criminology, Annee 1963 (1 Semestre), Paris: 58. With respect to the penal system as such, the Israeli experience illustrates that the management problem is found in many parts of the world and also occurs in a new country even when the leadership of the system is recruited from circles heavily influenced by humane and welfare causes. The nature of the task to which a prison system must address itself tends to modify these values. In this respect, the Israeli penal system represents a highly useful laboratory for the examination of general questions of administrative policy that must be examined in the light of the existing alternatives and the probable consequences. This laboratory is particularly well suited to the study of questions such as these.

The Israeli penal system represents a laboratory available for the examination of general policy questions that remain unanswered, such as:

1. Israel's penal system and network of punishments are humane. How does this fact affect the state of law and order?

2. The units of the system are small, with a potential for informal and personalized management. What are the consequences of this fact for the prison community, for inmates and for staff?

3. The control of criminals relies on sanctions that are relatively inexpensive to enforce, with very limited use of imprisonment which requires the expenditure of relatively large tax funds. This fact permits one to study such problems of punishment as:

    a. How do alternate punishments deter or fail to influence the subsequent behavior of offenders?

    b. What is the meaning of punishing a convicted offender, for those directly concerned with this offense, for the victim and for the general public?

    c. What are the risks to public safety inherent in a compassionate policy?

4. What are the administrative consequences of having decentralized law enforcement? Penal functions are handled by several ministries. Probation officers, for instance, are Ministry of Social Welfare employees. They are not dependent on judges, who are in the Ministry of Justice.

5. What is the impact on recidivism of having no statewide adult parole service?

In Israel, as in most democratic countries, judicial acts in criminal cases enforce social control through a highly variable and individualized treatment of offenses and offenders. When a crime is committed, the *crime* rather than the criminal or the victim is of concern to the law. Once courts have decided on the question of guilt, there is a shift of emphasis. The *criminal* rather than his act becomes the primary focus of the judicial process. This great humanistic experiment goes on each day and each year. Its outcome remains the subject of guesswork and speculation. Much of the data are at hand. They are carefully recorded in official proceedings that accompany each trial. What is needed in addition are systematically accumulated data regarding the results of imprisonment. These facts are not being collected for research analysis.

As a result, no one knows much about the consequences of the reform policies epitomized by Israel's penal system. But those who would do away with selective leniency rarely confront the consequences of more punitive alternatives. If Israel were to impose the sentences widely used

51

in the United States, the number of prisons might well have to be doubled or tripled, with related increases in welfare payments to the families of the criminals. More secure buildings and more trained staff would be required to incarcerate larger numbers of persons for longer periods of time. Such added expenditures would be hard to justify without careful evidence to demonstrate why they are in the public interest.

At the same time, Israel's compassionate orientation, while intriguing to penologists who study such questions, will remain subject to challenge because of the absence of information on the consequences of this approach.

Policy and the National Ethos

The security emphasis in Israel's prisons bears an intimate relationship to the general significance of safety in a country that has never known declared peace since its establishment. While there are few ordinary criminals who need rigid controls, and many inmates are released after short terms of imprisonment, most inmates are kept under medium- and close-custody conditions.

Prisons are expected to receive deviants who have not been dealt with satisfactorily by other well-established institutions. As a result, they often face questions for which no one has an answer. Policy makers are expected to make educated guesses in the face of considerable uncertainty. In Israel this difficulty is faced publicly. It is the object of much self-searching discussion among penological experts.

Consistent with the country's general emphasis on social planning, Israel has welcomed penal innovation, but it occurs within a conservative framework. In part, this reflects the fact that the correctional movement is primarily composed of prison officials. They are civil servants and therefore are limited in their freedom to advocate a controversial point of view.

The Scientific Social Movement Pattern

In an earlier study of penal reform in California the writer found it analytically useful to examine administrative changes as a pattern of overlapping stages that are characteristic of social movements.[4] Reforms were preceded by events that constituted a crisis. They were followed by incubation processes, initiation events, institutionalization procedures, formalism and decay indications and reorganization. To what extent is it useful to apply this pattern to the emergence of penal policy in Israel?

The career men determining prison policy did not begin their work

4. Joseph W. Eaton, *op. cit.,* 24-43.

life as penologists. Prisons are a subsidiary rather than a primary focus of their idealistic aspirations. The majority are deeply identified with a broader reformatory cause, the Zionist movement of rebuilding a Jewish national home within a progressive, creative and secure state. Law enforcement and the administration of prisons have become their particular assignment. They accept many of the principles of the worldwide correctional reform movement, but their subscription to this principle is ancillary rather than primary. The management of criminal deviants is, however, increasingly accepted as an important task — among a multitude of other assignments — in the process of building a modern state capable of supporting its present population and the immigrants who arrive in a steady stream each week.

The Zionist movement as a whole shows the developmental pattern of all social movements. Charismatic leaders hold the key posts of government, which, however, is becoming increasingly institutionalized. There are symptoms of formalism and decay, as well as of reorganization. Some practices that began as reforms and became static are being revitalized.

Within this larger social and ideological setting, the prison system is at an early state of institutional development. Its periods of major policy change were preceded by crises that reflected widespread dissatisfaction with the *status quo*. Public opinion was favorable to change. Those who supported the old order were placed on the defensive. When Israel became independent, all British prison officials and policy makers had to leave the country. A completely new policy was instituted to reflect the ethos of the new state. Similarly, the prison break at Shatta in 1958, which was viewed as a major crisis, led to a reversal of organizational priorities. Security precautions gained in ascendancy over treatment objectives.

Each crisis has been followed by a phase of administrative stabilization. Officials are exploring alternate administrative arrangements to accomplish their various objectives. There is as yet no full-blown comprehensive reform program that is being pursued through long-range planning. Israel's penal policy is fluid. Divergent points of view are allowed to co-exist at top policy levels. No one seems to be ready to disregard the consideration of program alternatives. Young men and women with primary professional career aspirations in criminology and in prison rehabilitation are just beginning to be available in small numbers.

The prison system exists within a country in which experimentation and pioneering pervade many governmental and voluntary programs. The spirit of innovation flourishes in the administration of justice outside and behind prison walls. This spirit is an antidote to the conservative tendency of most large bureaucracies: maximization of stability and predictability by settling for a *status quo* in which fundamental questions can no longer be seriously entertained. Penal questions are being asked in Israel. And questioning provides the basis for hope that some more definitive answers can be found.

Index

Arab Israelis: 22-23

Bachi, R.: 19
Bar-Ilan University: 9
Ben Aharon, Y.: 35
Ben-Gurion, David — quoted: 23
Ben Zvi, Yitchak: 8
Breazeale, C. E.: 32

Chalutzim: 40
Churchill, Winston — quoted: xiii
Cohn, Haim — quoted: 27-28, 29
Crime and criminals: 5-7, 18-21, 27-28, 29; statistics: 19, 20, 21, 23-25, 31, 34
Criminal Code Ordinances (1936): 3
Criminal law: 3-4, 7-8

Damoun Prison: 14, 16-18
Drapkin, Israel — quoted: 13

Eichmann, Adolf: 6
Etzioni, Moshe: 35

Feddahin: 34
Fenton, Norman: 38
Finance, Ministry of: 7
Fitzgerald, Edmond: ix-x, 7, 9, 12

Geyra, Gero: 11

Haganah: 2
Hebrew University: 9, 50
Hermon, Zvi: 12, 37
Herzl, Theodor: 10-11
Human relations specialists: x-xi, 40-41

Immigrants: 2-3, 11, 18-19
Imprisonment: 23-28, 38-40
International Society of Criminology: 50
Israeli Institute for Applied Social Research: 9

Jaffe, Lester — quoted: 30-31
Jerusalem Post — quoted: 35
Jewish national fund: 1
Judges: 24, 26
Justice, Minister of: 7, 50
Justice, Ministry of: 3-4, 9
Juvenile delinquency: 19

Juvenile Offender Ordinance (1947): 3-4

Kibbutzim: 19
Klebanoff, Y.: 35

Law reforms: 7-8
Law of Return: 2-3

Massiyahu Camp: 14
Military pioneers: x-xi, 40
Millo, E.: 19
Ministries. See name of Ministry, as Justice, Ministry of.

National Council for the Prevention of Crime and Delinquency: 4, 42
Neve Tirza: 14
Nir, Aryeh: 18, 37
Nissim, Victoria: 38

Police, Minister of: 8
Police, Ministry of: 3-4
Police Ordinances: 3
Prison conditions: xii-xiii, 13, 14-18, 21, 23-24
Prison employees: 2
Prison furloughs: 31-32
Prison Ordinance (1946): 3-4
Prison organization: vii, ix
Prisoners — education and training: 15, 17, 26; statistics: 1-2, 36; treatment: 27, 30-31, 33, 37, 38
Prisons — costs: 11-12, 28; criticisms of: 42-43; policy: 43-47; security: 35-38, 41-45, 52
Probation Offender Ordinance (1944): 3-4

Rachmanuth: 5
Ramle Prison: 14-16
Recidivism: 30-31
Release Board: 7-8
Rosner, David: 27

Samuel, Edwin — quoted: 3
Scalia, M. B. — quoted: 9-10
Sentences: 23-26, 28-31

55